THE MATURE MIND

Books by H. A. Overstreet

ABOUT OURSELVES

INFLUENCING HUMAN BEHAVIOR

OUR FREE MINDS

A DECLARATION OF INTERDEPENDENCE

THE MATURE MIND

THE
MATURE
MIND

H. A. OVERSTREET

W · W · NORTON *&* COMPANY · INC ·
NEW YORK

TO
B. W. O.

CONTENTS

PREFACE

M ANKIND," wrote Alfred North Whitehead, "is now in one of its rare moods of shifting its outlook. The mere compulsion of tradition has lost its force. It is the business of philosophers, students and practical men to re-create and re-enact a vision of the world, conservative and radical, including those elements of reverence and order without which society lapses into a riot, a vision penetrated through and through with unflinching rationality."

This book concerns the re-creation and re-enactment of such a vision through an insight that comes chiefly out of the psychological and psychiatric sciences and centers in man's mental, emotional, and social maturing. As this new insight penetrates our common consciousness, it helps us to understand the forces that have created our predicaments and brought us close to destruction; and it affords the clue to our possible advance out of chaos.

This insight is what I choose to call the maturity concept. The understanding and living out of this most recent of our psychological and philosophic insights becomes our next obligation and hope.

I wish to express my gratitude to numerous fellow scientists and philosophers for help they have given me—help that most of them do not even know they have given. More personally, I wish to thank my wife, Bonaro W. Overstreet; my son, Alan Burr Overstreet; and his wife, Jeanne.

H. A. O.

PART ONE

THE MATURITY CONCEPT

ONE

PSYCHOLOGICAL FOUNDATIONS

THE CHARACTERISTIC knowledge of our century is psychological. Even the most dramatic advances in physics and chemistry are chiefly applications of known methods of research. But the attitude toward human nature and human experience that has come in our time is new.

This attitude could not have come earlier. Before it came, there had to be long preparation. Physiology had to be a developed science; for the psychological person is also physiological. His mind, among other things, is a matter of brain tissue, of nerves, of glands, of organs of touch, smell, and sight. It was not until about seventy years ago that physiology was sufficiently developed to make psychophysical research possible, as in the laboratories of the distinguished German psychologist, William Wundt. But before physiology there had to be a developed science of biology. Since brain, nerves, glands, and the rest all depend upon cell processes, the science of the living cell had to have its maturing before a competent physiology could emerge.

But before biology there had to be chemistry; and before chemistry, physics; and before physics, mathematics. So the long preparation goes back into the centuries.

There is, in short, a time clock of science. Each science has to wait until its hour strikes. Today, at last, the time clock of science strikes the hour of psychology; and a new enlightenment begins.

To be sure, the interests explored by this latest of the sciences are themselves old; but the accuracy of research is new. There is, in brief, a kind of iron logic that is in control. Each science has to wait for its peculiar accuracy until its predecessor has supplied the data and tools out of which its accuracy can be made.

Today this new psychological accuracy is bringing insights that are remaking our life. One insight in particular is of such commanding import that it may be said to be the master concept of our time. This is the concept of psychological maturity.

We have known in a way about psychological maturity—but vaguely and intermittently. Its full meaning now begins to dawn upon us. As it begins to dawn, we realize that the maturity concept is central to our whole enterprise of living. This is what our past wisdoms have been leading up to. This, it would seem, is what we must now accept if we are to move forward out of the confusions and despairs of our day.

The time clock of science has struck a new hour; and a new insight begins to be at our service.

II

All children, Diderot once observed, are essentially criminal. It is merely our good luck that their physical powers are still too limited to permit them to carry out their destructiveness.

Had he lived today, Diderot might have expanded his remark. He might have said that all childish minds are dangerous, but particularly when those minds are housed in adult bodies; for then they have the power to put their immaturities fully and disastrously into effect.

The forms that adult childishness can take are almost infinite in number. They exist not merely in those unfortunates who have to be confined to institutions, but in countless thousands of men and women who look adult, are taken to be adult, and are granted the full prerogatives of adulthood.

In these grown-up child-minds, the immaturities are almost invariably disguised from the individuals themselves. Also they are usually disguised from those who share their life—largely because these others display similar immaturities themselves. The immaturities, moreover, are disguised from society at large, since that society has as yet developed no constant habit of appraising adult behaviors as immature or mature.

Once, however, we begin to understand these immaturities in adults, we have a clue as to how to bring into our human affairs a greater measure of sanity. The immaturities explain much in our history for which we have hitherto had no sufficient explanation. Similarly, they explain many baffling facts about our present-day behavior, both private and public. They offer us, therefore, a key with which to unlock stubborn problems that have to do with our common welfare and our personal happiness.

Also, they provide us with a hope. For these immaturities, fixed as they seem to be in many adults, and powerful as they are in many institutions, are themselves subject to change. Something can be done about them. At the least they can be recognized for what they are and their influence thus lessened. But more than that, the conditions that bring them about and that encourage their continuance can themselves be altered. Both in our private lives and in the social life of our times, we can begin to do a new thing: we can put a premium upon psychological maturity.

To put that premium upon adult maturity is our next great concern.

III

Obviously, the maturity concept is not something that has been made out of whole cloth. It is the outgrowth of the major psychological and psychiatric discoveries of our time. Out of the laboratories and the clinics there have come certain insights into our human nature that add up to what we are here calling the maturity concept. These insights are (1) the idea of psychological age; (2) the idea of arrested development or fixation; (3) the idea of conditioned response; (4) the idea of aptitude uniqueness; and (5) the idea of adult capacity to learn. When the significance of these five insights is caught and interpreted, they point to one fact: that the proper psychological undertaking of man is to move from immaturity toward maturity.

The first of these insights is the idea of psychological age. This idea came into initial use through the efforts of Binet, at the turn of the century, to measure the mental age of children. What he attempted had never been done before. It had long been recognized, of course, that some children are "brighter" than others; but there had been no successful attempt to relate brightness or dullness to the age of the child. Through experiments with thousands of children, Binet was able to establish the fact that there are norms of accomplishment for the different ages of childhood. At a certain chronological age, for example, the "normal" child can be expected to put a square block into a square hole and a round block into a round hole. If at that age a child is still unable to do the expected thing, he is retarded. That is, he is younger on the scale of mental growth than he is on the scale of physical growth. If, on the contrary, he can already do what only older children are normally able to do, he can be rated as above his age—as older in mental terms than in physical.

Thus it came to be seen that psychological age need by no means correspond to chronological age. A boy ten years old by the solar calendar may be only five years old by his psychological calendar; or he may be fifteen.

This insight immediately placed a new responsibility upon educators. They could no longer indiscriminately lump children together. A psychological four-year-old who was chronologically ten years of age could not possibly keep pace with a class of ten-year-olds. To expect him to do so was arbitrarily to condemn him to failure. Nor could a psychological fifteen-year-old who was chronologically ten be safely treated in exactly the same way as those who more closely fitted the average ten-year-old pattern. Unless provision was made for differences of psychological age, the "below age" child would be driven by despair into apathy or antisocial behaviors; the "above age" child would "go nuts" with boredom and would, in all likelihood, emerge from his schooling with more contempt than respect for the ordinary human race of which he was, in the specific area of mental growth, an extraordinary member.

Obviously, something new had here been brought to our attention: an insight into our human nature which had, once for all, made it obligatory that we look at people with new eyes. It was established that every individual has a psychological as well as a chronological age. Since Binet's day, this insight has been so cultivated that the measurement of psychological age has now become standard practice. Too often, however, even where the most conscientious techniques of measurement are employed, the full significance of the concept of psychological age is not grasped. It is understood that here is a means of more effectively classifying children for their school work; it is not always understood that here is an insight that reveals our human nature as possessed of hitherto unsuspected dimensions of complexity.

Binet started with the measurement of the mental age of the child: his power to solve problems. Later psychologists extended their exploration into the emotional and social areas of the individual's life. Here, too, it was discovered, psychological age may differ markedly from chronological. A woman of thirty, say, is found to be on the emotional level of the average fifteen-year-old. Chronologically, she is an adult; but her emotional reactions are still those characteristic of adolescence. Or a boy of ten is found to have a sense of responsibility and a steadiness of purpose that go normally with twenty years. Chronologically a child, he is emotionally an adult. In like manner, explorations have been made to estimate degrees of social maturity. A man of twenty-five may have the ego-centered outlook of a typical five-year-old; or a child of five may be far beyond his playmates of his own age in his power of give and take, his sense of justice, and his spontaneous helpfulness.

All of this has provided a new approach to our human selves. The essential thing about an individual, we are being brought to realize, is not so much the number of years he has lived as the psychological competence that those years have netted him. Thus we are given a new way to estimate ourselves and others. *Not all adults are adult.* Many who look grown-up on the outside may be childish on the inside. Others who look childish on the outside may be surprisingly mature on the the inside. Psychological age, moreover, as distinct from chronological, is not merely an academic curiosity. Whether a person is average, advanced, or retarded in his mental, emotional, and social growth may be the concealed reason— and the chief reason—why his adult relationships with his world are as they are.

That we have by no means fully learned the significance of

this insight is indicated by the fact that, except in the case of imbeciles and morons, we still admit people to all the major prerogatives of life on a purely chronological basis. The age at which schooling begins and ends is chronological; so is the age at which people may marry without parental consent; so is the age at which they are considered ready for responsible work; so is the age at which they can vote and hold office. After the members of our society have gained enough years to be rated as legally adult, society, except in the most flagrant cases, exercises no control over their daily exhibitions of immaturity.

But as we become more fully aware that chronological age does not necessarily betoken a corresponding emotional or social age, we can go seriously at the task of devising ways in which crass immaturity among adults—particularly among those in places of power—may be detected. Up to this date in human history we have had no accurate way of estimating the psychological maturity of a Congressman, say, or of a judge, or of a superintendent of schools, or of a teacher, or of the head of a corporation. Psychologically, in brief, we have flown blind. Precisely because the motives that carry individuals to positions of influence may range all the way from the infantile to the finely mature, we have had power exerted on the adult level by individuals of almost every conceivable psychological age. Side by side in the halls of Congress, in college faculty meetings, in church, in citizens' committees— and everywhere else where people congregate—we have had the immature and the mature.

The concept of psychological age has only begun to enter

our common consciousness. We are generally familiar with its application to children, but we are only beginning to be alert to behavior symptoms in grown men and women that should warn us of their psychological immaturity; that should warn us, for example, against giving them a major chance to set the success standards of our society or to exert power over other people's lives. Also, we are only now beginning to ask how psychological immaturity can be overcome. We are only beginning, but this new psychological way of regarding ourselves and our human fellows is definitely on the books. When it is also definitely and clearly in our consciousness, we may be set for such a new appraisal of human behaviors as will preface a new society.

I V

The second clarifying idea—that of arrested development, or fixation—had its inception in the epoch-making work of Freud. He set out to discover the causes of certain diseases that had baffled medical science for centuries—and that had baffled him in his own medical practice. These diseases presented physical symptoms, yet they stubbornly refused to yield to physical treatment: paralyses that were not "true" paralyses, blindnesses not marked by tissue deterioration, vomitings, tremors, tics, amnesias, deafnesses, deliriums, phobias, obsessions, compulsions.

Working first with hypnosis, then combining it with "mental catharsis" or "talking out," and later discarding hypnosis entirely, Freud probed into the personality-depths of his patients. In a way unprecedented in medical practice, he let his

patients talk themselves out, encouraging them to say anything that came into their minds, encouraging them in particular to recover the lost memories of their childhood. Out
of this came his epochal discovery that many of the baffling
diseases of adulthood had psychic origins—in unresolved
emotional conflicts of childhood.

The key idea was that of "unresolved emotional conflict."
Where a child, he discovered, had undergone some wrenching experience that threatened its basic emotional security;
where the child could not, because of its immaturity, understand the experience and take it in its stride; and where, because of some taboo, it was not permitted to talk out its
problem with its parents, there was the likelihood that an
inner conflict would remain unresolved. Instead of passing
into the normal life-stream and aiding the child in his growth
toward maturity, this unnegotiable experience would be repressed into the unconscious. There it would remain fixated
as a deep sense of guilt or incompetence; and from there it
would operate as the source of later emotional disturbances.

Freud's method of cure was to get the patient, through a
prolonged and seemingly irrelevant process of talking out his
life, to revive the memory of this repressed and long-forgotten
shock experience. When the revival finally did take place—
when the child's unnegotiable experience was at last placed
within the context of adult understanding—the conflict was
resolved and the patient cured.

A vast amount of controversy has ensued since Freud let
his first neurotic patients talk themselves out. Freud himself
built out of the revelations brought forth by his simple but

amazingly effective technique a whole system of psychology that has been variously attacked and defended: accepted *in toto* by some psychiatrists and greatly modified by others. We are not interested, here, in Freudianism as a total system, but rather in a single Freudian insight that seems to be unassailable and that profoundly illumines the problem of man's maturing. This is the insight that whenever, in the formative years of life, an intense emotional conflict is left unresolved, it does not disappear but remains as a festering element that later takes the form of a severe emotional disturbance or of a of a pervasive uneasiness in the handling of life.

What this insight comes to, in its simplicity, is that a human being does not grow beyond a problem that has deep emotional significance for him until he comes to terms with that problem: until he understands it; accommodates it in his life arrangements; if possible, resolves it entirely. Instead of growing beyond such an unresolved problem—and of growing beyond its power to hurt—the individual becomes fixated at the point of development where he encountered the problem. A neurosis in adulthood is a sign that at some certain point in the formative years of life development was thus arrested. A shock experience that should properly have been assimilated and outlived was, instead, repressed into the unconscious, where it continued to operate in its infantile form. The adult, in brief, is neurotic because he is continuing to seek in infantile ways a solution to a problem that overpowered him in infancy. Thus, a neurosis is an ungrown-up way of trying to solve a conflict that can only be solved, by the adult, in a grown-up way.

Not all immature adults are neurotic; but where there is adult immaturity this same pattern of arrested development, or fixation, is likely to show up as the root cause for the halting of the maturing process. Mental, emotional, and social immaturity in an adult is not, in short, an inexplicable mystery: not since Freud. Such immaturity indicates that the adult is still trying to work out *by childish means* the problem of his various relationships to life.

We may illustrate by a familiar example. Early in life, a child may learn that he can get what he wants by making a nuisance of himself. If he will scream loudly enough, kick his heels, hold his breath, choke, get red in the face, he can frighten the life out of his parents and make them yield. It does not take a child long to become wise to this way of solving his problem—that of a conflict of desires between himself and his parents. A "mature" solution of such a conflict would involve a mutual talking out of the situation and the reaching of an agreement. This, clearly, is as yet impossible to the child; so he seeks to get what he wants by the only means that seem within his command and that get results.

If the child has wise parents, he may be helped to outgrow this infantile way of attacking a problem. They may be able, in their wisdom, to perform the double act of refusing to yield to his methods of "persuasion" and yet of giving him so deep a sense of their love and dependability that he can risk reliance upon their care and can gradually mature his methods of satisfying his wants.

If the child has unwise parents who, time after time, give in to him—or who, by their own erratic moods, keep him insecure—his infantile way of going at problems may well become fixed in him; and he may be thus arrested in his proper development toward mature problem-solving. Should this happen, he may be found at forty, say, as a man who still gets his own way by having tantrums; browbeating his wife; terrifying his children; bawling out his subordinates. If he happens to be in politics, instead of trying to explore political issues to their rational depths, he may simply wear down his opponents by a method equivalent to the childish method of screaming and kicking his heels.

A comparable though quite different case of arrested development is that of the adult practical joker. Somewhere along the line, this individual found that he could get importance or significance for himself by making someone else look foolish—and he made that discovery at so early an age that he did not yet have the kind of social imagination that would make him feel keenly the other person's hurt. Having achieved success in attention-getting through the use of a preadult method, he clings to that method—so that at forty he wears a squirt-bulb flower in his lapel, hands out firecracker cigars, rigs up a friend's car so that a small torpedo will explode when the car is started, and rips up hotel furniture during a Legion convention. Paunchy and bald, and with the laugh of vacuous triumph, he remains to the end of his days the small boy who has never grown up.

This insight into the causes of arrested development, or fixation, is of prime importance to our understanding of maturity. In the first place, it focuses our attention upon the formative years of life. Survival is a child's first need; a sense of his own significance is the second. The child, from birth, needs to feel secure; needs to be noticed; needs to be wanted. These deep, inescapable needs are frequently not satisfied. In all kinds of ways, the child may be made to feel that he amounts to nothing, that he is a nuisance, a drag, a failure, an unwanted member of the family. No child can stand that. Thus slapped down, he has to find some way to win attention and significance. If he were mature, he could attack his problem by developing a competence and by establishing personal relationships with people outside his own family. But he is immature: that is, he is helpless either to understand his problem or to solve it by rational means. Thus he does the only thing he can do: he tries to resolve it by the means at his command, and these, by the nature of things, are immature means. He may get what he wants by aggressiveness— if his trials in that direction bring him success. Or he may retreat into fantasy, building the habit of seeing himself a hero in every situation and of seeing other people as incapable of appreciating him. Or he may become outwardly submissive—at the same time developing unconscious hostilities that he cannot acknowledge even to himself. Gearing his life to such immature methods of problem-solving, he unwittingly halts his own growth toward emotional and social maturity.

An insight that thus focuses attention upon the formative years can mean much for the advance of our civilization. If a fine maturity is rare among adults, one chief reason, we begin to see, lies in our hitherto widespread ignorance of the thousand and one ways in which the maturing process can be checked in the early years of life. If we want a greater maturity among the adults of the future, the years of infancy and childhood—and the emotional problems that mark those years—deserve every wise attention they can be given.

A second importance of this insight is that it helps us to discriminate, where the behavior of grownups is concerned, between what is genuinely mature and what is infantile. We begin to add a new keenness to our social intelligence as we learn to ask the question, "Is this man (or woman) solving his problems in an adult or in an infantile manner?"

A third importance follows: we begin to look about for ways in which to re-establish the growth processes of such undeveloped adults. Where we see grownups missing out on the rich experience of maturity—or see them creating fear and misery for others—we can no longer be satisfied to say, "Oh, he's only a grown-up boy," or "She's really a little girl at heart." Knowing that "little boys and girls" who have adult bodies and adult power can do vast mischief in a world that desperately needs maturity, we begin to ask how these oversized "little ones" can be encouraged to act their age. We begin to ask, moreover, what family practices, classroom practices, and various cultural practices have thus far discouraged their acting their age.

This insight into arrested development or fixation, in short, makes us take a new look at the whole process of human growth, from birth to death—through infancy, childhood, adolescence, adulthood. It makes us aware of "fateful" years of life and of "fateful" experiences. It induces in us a new seriousness about how life should develop.

V

In the early nineteen hundreds, a Russian physiologist, Ivan Pavlov, performed an experiment on a dog. It looked like a simple, routine experiment—the kind that thousands of physiologists perform every day. But this experiment was not routine in its consequences. It was seminal. Out of it came a new comprehension of what makes us become the creatures we are and of what can make us become very different creatures.

The experiment of the dog, the meat, and the bell is too well known now to require retelling. The point of it lay in what Pavlov discovered about the manner in which artificial stimuli can become incorporated into our natural make-up. To salivate when meat is brought is "natural" to a dog. But no one, a priori, would suppose that a dog would salivate because a bell was rung. Yet by ringing a bell every time the meat was brought, Pavlov was able so to "condition" dog-nature that salivation took place merely at the ringing of the bell, without the presence of meat. Out of this and succeeding experiments the idea of the *conditioned response* entered the thinking of our century; and it has become one more of the major ideas out of which our *maturity concept* can be shaped.

One thing it has shown us is that man's nature—like the dog's nature—is not something fixed and unalterable. Amazing things can be done to make it different from its "natural" self. In all the centuries of canine life, there had never been a dog that had spontaneously salivated at the ringing of a bell;

for the ringing of a bell has nothing to do with the physiological process of salivation. Yet by a few repetitions of bell-and-meat-together, a certain dog, in the early nineteen hundreds, was turned into a hitherto unknown kind of creature. Where hitherto he (like all his canine fellows) had been only meat-responding, he was now turned into a unique being—a dog that was bell-responding.

What was found to be true of the dog was easily shown to be true of man. Man, in innumerable ways, can be conditioned to be a creature that he is not by his original nature. He is not by his original nature, for example, a creature who spontaneously stops his forward movement when a red light appears. Yet, as we know, he can be made into that kind of creature. Similarly, he can be conditioned to eat spinach and like it; to kill his fellow men and feel proud of it; to insult a minority race and feel justified in his discourtesy. In each case, the result is accomplished by the "meat-and-bell" process. The eating of spinach wins him approving smiles; the killing of fellow men is accompanied by citations, medals, the cheers of the multitude; the discourtesy to a minority race is lauded as a solicitude for race purity. In each case, an artificial stimulus is so closely tied up with the satisfaction of a basic need—for food, safety, approval, a sense of belonging —that response to the stimulus is felt as "natural."

Within limits, in brief, the human being can become almost anything that is conceived as desirable by those who set up the stimuli to which he responds. We cannot make man into an airplane; but we can make him into an airplane-maker. We cannot make him into an atomic bomb; but we can make him into a creature who feels it necessary to make and use an atomic bomb. Within the limits of our human nature reside almost limitless possibilities. What we have thus far made of ourselves, during all the millennia of our history on earth, is only a preliminary to what we may make of ourselves. Apply the proper stimuli and the old Adam can be turned into the new Adam.

This is the rousing news brought to us by Pavlov's experiments on conditioned response. It is news, however, that cuts both ways: by effective stimuli we can build far more enlightened and capable human beings; but by equally effective stimuli, we can build creatures in whom human powers are dangerously distorted. In the schools that Hitler designed for German youth, for example, the "meat-and-bell" technique conditioned a whole generation of boys and girls to contempt for non-Aryans, to cruelty to Jews, to spying upon parents and neighbors, to unquestioning obedience to the Fuehrer. The Nazi youth—male and female—who poured like a scourge over Europe, had been conditioned into creatures unrecognizable as human by common standards of human decency.

This is one way in which conditioning can work—and it is a way that we are learning to worry about. All through our human society—in families, schools, communities, nations—a vast amount of conditioning is taking place that is inimical to maturity; that is inimical, even, to human survival.

In the modern world, for example, most of the earth's inhabitants have been conditioned to the concept of nationalism. A man may be a man "for a' that"; but first of all, he is an American, a Russian, a German. We might more properly

say, in the light of Pavlov's experiment, that modern man
was born human, but that by a complex, reiterated "meat-and-
bell" technique he has been made into an American, a Russian, a German. That is to say, he has been brought to the
point where he spontaneously associates the satisfaction of
his own needs with the strength and permanence of his own
nation. The experience of belonging to that nation is, in fact,
of such psychic importance to him that he will seek to pre-
serve it even at the risk of his life. One of the most interesting
psychological events of our time is that a new "meat-and-
bell" setup is beginning to challenge the old: little by little,
through the presence of new stimulating facts, man is being
persuaded to bring into spontaneous association the satisfaction of his own needs and the idea of one world. That is, his
natural need to belong is being related to a different object:
not the tribe, or the nation, but a united mankind. If this new
conditioned linkage is firmly established, so that the average
individual is as deeply moved by feeling himself a citizen
of the world as he has long been moved by feeling himself a
citizen of a nation, the change will have taken place by a
process that Pavlov made familiar. The difference between
provincial man and cosmopolitan man will be, in a sense,
analogous to the difference between the meat-responding
dog and the bell-responding dog.

Happily, however, the difference will be of greater moment than a mere statement of that analogy would imply.
Cosmopolitan man will, in contrast to provincial man, be
man with a greater chance to mature; man with a larger area
in which he can exercise his faculty for fairness and reason-

ableness without coming up against fixed loyalty-barriers that bid him stop. We shall have more to say, later, about the types of political arrangement that make for immaturity and for maturity. Here it is sufficient to say that Pavlov, when he introduced his insight regarding conditioned responses, gave us one more clue both as to why many people grow to adulthood without becoming psychologically mature and as to how we can begin to work for the further maturing of our human race. Maturity is achieved where conditions favorable to maturity exist: that is the clue.

V I

A fourth seminal insight of modern psychology is the idea of individual uniqueness. In one sense, of course, this is not a new insight: all our great social and philosophical thinkers have been keenly aware of the fact of individual differences. It has remained, however, for psychologists to give the insight scientific precision.

As far back as 1885, the psychologist, Carl Stumpf, began work on tests of musical talent. Since that time, other psychologists—Revecz, Rupp, Seashore, Lowery, Schoen, Kwallwasser, Dykema, Drake, Ortman, and others—have tried to isolate this particular uniqueness in individuals and measure its strength. Clearly, with respect to musical talent, all individuals were by no means alike. Some appeared to have no musical aptitude whatever; others were highly endowed with power to appreciate musical tones and rhythms and to create in their forms.

The test of musical ability was only the beginning. Soon

it was seen that there was another specific aptitude in which individuals differed: namely, mechanical aptitude. Researches to isolate and measure this particular talent were begun. As a result, numerous tests have been devised to distinguish the mechanical genius from the mechanical dub. In like manner, clerical aptitudes have been isolated and measured with a fair amount of success. Attempts have also been made, though with less success so far, to measure medical and artistic aptitudes.

What all this adds up to is more than just a working body of information about this and that skill. It adds up to a basic recognition of one important factor in the maturing of the individual. If each individual has a certain uniqueness of power, his maturing will best be accomplished along the line of that power. To try to develop him along lines that go in directions contrary to that of his major strength is to condition him to defeat. Thus, the non-mechanical person who is arbitrarily thrust into a mechanical occupation cannot help but do his work poorly and reluctantly, with some deep part of himself in conscious or unconscious rebellion.

He may blame himself for the low level of his accomplishment or for his persistent discontent; but not all his self-berating, nor even all his efforts to become more competent by further training, can make up for the original aptitude-lack. Unless he discovers this aptitude-lack, he may be doomed to a lifetime of self-blame, with a consequent loss of self-confidence and a halting of his psychological growth.

Or he may take refuge in self-pity—finding reason to believe that his failure is due to one or another bad break, to the jealousy of a superior, to lack of sympathy and help at home, to an initial bad start, to a lack of appreciation of what he does. If he thus goes the way of self-pity, he is doomed to a lifetime of self-commiseration that makes sound growth impossible.

Or he may go the way of general hostility without ever tracing this hostility to its source in his work-life. If he is, for example, one of those unhappy modern workers who have come to accept their daily labor as a source of income only, and who do not expect it to yield satisfaction in its own right, it may never occur to him that there is a relationship between his quick angers and fixed prejudices, on the one hand, and his misplacement in work, on the other. Yet that misplacement may be the most distorting factor in his experience— and the most *inescapably* distorting, since it is with him every day.

Once the idea becomes central in our culture that a man is at his best when he is doing his best at what he can do best, many of the present hindrances to a sound maturing will be removed. To mature is to bring one's powers to realization. To waste those powers, or to force individuals to try to exhibit powers they do not possess, is to defeat the maturing impulse of life.

This point of view about aptitude is of special importance to the schools. In the main, schools have been a kind of aptitude melting pot. All the different special strengths of individual students have been thrown in together and melted down into an undifferentiated mass. With this new insight, however—and the tests that now support it—the years of schooling, from nursery school to adult education, can become years, not of flattening out the individual into the "average," but of building him up into the uniqueness of his own powers. As more and more members of our society are thus built up, we will have as a cultural asset more and more people who enjoy the processes that lead to maturity and who begin to glimpse the fact that the movement toward maturity is the movement toward happiness.

The characteristic of the mature person is that he affirms life. To affirm life he must be involved, heart and soul, in the process of living. Neither the person who feels himself a failure nor the person who consciously or unconsciously resents what life has done to him can feel his heart and soul engaged in the process of living. That experience is reserved for the person whose full powers are enlisted. This, then, is what this fourth insight signifies: to mature, the individual must know what his powers are and must make them competent for life. Know thyself, said Socrates. Know your aptitudes, say these modern Socratics.

VII

In 1928, Edward Thorndike published a book, *Adult Learning*, which reversed a long established assumption: namely, that childhood is the time of learning; that adulthood is the time of *having learned*.

Because of this ancient assumption the educational energies of the American people had been largely expended on the building of public schools for children and young people. The hope was that if all the young of America could be educated, the destinies of a democratic nation would be made secure. Where the young were not properly schooled, they were commonly taken to be "lost" so far as their education was concerned: adult minds were too old and stiff to be learning-minds. The accepted pronouncement was that you can't teach an old dog new tricks.

The establishment of adult education in America did not wait upon psychological research. Here, as in every other field, there were individuals of creative insight who saw in human nature much that was concealed from the average view. Even before Thorndike conducted his investigations and published his book, many pioneering ventures had grown up to independent strength and had federated into an American adult education movement. But again it was the psychologist who gave the scientific basis for what had already been done by trial and error; and it was the psychologist who so set forth facts regarding the *how* and *why* of adult learning that those facts could become naturalized in the common mind.

Based on an exhaustive examination of psychological data and on various specifically devised experiments with adult groups, Thorndike's book announced as its established conclusion the fact that adults can learn. "In general, nobody under forty-five should restrain himself from trying to learn anything because of a belief or fear that he is too old to be able to learn. Nor should he use that fear as an excuse for not learning anything which he ought to learn. If he fails in learning it, inability due directly to age will very rarely, if ever, be the reason." [1]

The actual reason why adults do not see themselves as learners, he pointed out, is that factors either *within themselves* or *within their culture* place certain obstacles in the way. The factors *within themselves* may be various: a lack of aptitude for learning the particular subject undertaken; a desire too weak to establish proper attention-habits where the habits are absent; ignorance of how to set about learning; habits, ideas, or emotional tendencies that block the learning experience. Obstacles *within the culture* arise from the *unusualness* of adult study: from the fact that the enterprise of organized learning lies outside the accustomed pattern of adult life. There is the possibility of ridicule; of being made conspicuous by "going to school" when grownups are supposed to be through with school; of loneliness in an experience that was a companionable one during the years of childhood; of being thought inferior or stupid by seeming to need to study at an age when study is presumed to have been accomplished. It is, Thorndike established once for all, factors like these—personal and cultural—that discourage adult learning. It is not adulthood itself.

For a people who had placidly accepted the immaturity of non-learning, this was a sharp alert. If adults did not learn, it was not the fault of nature. To justify the dying back of their brains by the fact that they were grown men and women would no longer do. Where there was aliveness of interest and

---

[1] Edward L. Thorndike, *Adult Learning*, p. 177. New York, The Macmillan Company.

purpose, "growing old" might mean growing wiser in mind and character. It might also mean growing more informed in matters relating to personal and common welfare.

As other psychologists and educators have carried further what Thorndike began, it has become increasingly apparent, not only that adults can learn, but that it is a threat to our whole society to have them stop learning, to have them become fixed in an unhappy or a complacent unchangeability in a world where they are constantly confronted by the problem of change. "This is an age . . . of rapid evolution and sometimes revolution in politics and economics as well as technology. Facts and ideas that were right yesterday may be wrong or completely irrelevant today. An adult who ceases after youth to unlearn and relearn his facts and to reconsider his opinions is like a blindfolded person walking into a familiar room where someone has moved the furniture. Furthermore he is a menace to a democratic community. One of the consequences of a rapidly changing world is that there is a much more important job for adult education than ever before. In fact, adult education in these days should rank in importance with elementary, secondary, and college education." [2]

Here, then, is a fifth psychological contribution to the *maturity concept*. Whether or not old dogs can learn new tricks, old human beings can—and must—learn new facts and insights as long as they live.

[2] Eugene Staley, "Knowledge for Survival," in *California Journal of Elementary Education*, November 1947, p. 96.

VIII

Since the beginning of the modern age, the chief method of science has been that of dividing to conquer. By this method it has put at our disposal a well-nigh incredible body of facts regarding everything from the behavior of the atom to the behavior of the human mind confronted by a problem. We have amassed, as it were, an enormous stock pile of classified information. Now, apparently, science is ready for a new method: that of uniting to conquer. What has been divided and subdivided for purposes of research is now being reassembled for purposes of interpretation and of application to human affairs.

Even the newspapers have recognized it as news when atomic scientists, sociologists, and psychologists sit down together to try to fuse their separate brands of knowledge into wisdom about the future of man. Not less newsworthy—though it has not yet made the headlines—is the fact that within the separate disciplines a like process of reintegration is under way. Within the field of psychology, for example, the fragmented human being—fragmented for purposes of minute and accurate research—is being once more made whole. Explorations that have long seemed to lead in different directions are converging and taking a common road.

The *maturity concept* is one product of this new process of integration and synthesis. In it are brought together—for mutual illumination and pooled strength—the chief insights into human nature and behavior that have thus far been contributed by psychological and psychiatric science: insights that have hitherto stood, for the most part, in mutual isolation.

It has not been customary, for example, to talk in the same breath about Binet and Freud, or about Pavlov and Thorndike. It has not been customary to talk in the same breath about man as a creature of unique individual aptitudes and man as a creature fixated at the level of childhood by unresolved problems lodged in his unconscious. What now becomes unmistakably clear, however, is that all psychologists and psychiatrists who contribute true insights into the nature of man are talking about the same subject. They are talking about *man*. What one says, therefore, can scarcely be wholly irrelevant to what another says. What they all say becomes by common implication of prime importance to our task of creating a world suitable for the nature of man. What has been joined together in human nature can be put asunder only for purposes of research. Sooner or later, it must be rejoined for purposes of living.

When Binet announced that psychological growth does not automatically keep pace with physical growth, he was reporting on a specific, deliberately restricted set of experiments. Yet there is a telling connection between what he had to say and what Freud had to say about why emotional growth is so often halted long before physical adulthood is reached. Likewise, there is a connection between Freud's insight and Pavlov's studies of the conditioned response. Freud, for example, gave as one reason for arrested development the fact that various cultural taboos—such as sexual taboos—made it impossible for children to escape a sense of guilt; made it impossible for them to acknowledge their own natures. But the child's response to a taboo is a *conditioned response:* Pavlov threw clear light upon the process of its establishment.

The principle of the *conditioned response* is equally clarifying when we turn to Thorndike's analysis of why most adults shy away from organized learning: they have been brought up to believe that such learning belongs to childhood. When, moreover, Thorndike talks of those resistances to learning that exist *within the self,* we find quick reason to refer to what we have been taught by Freud and his followers. How often, for example, is the process of learning brought to an end because an individual is still acting out a childhood drama of dependence and submission—and is thus turned away from any genuine desire to become independent and competent? How often is the adult emotionally disqualified for a program of learning by the fact that he is making his sense of significance out of a childish aggressiveness that would make him unwilling to cast any other person in the role of teacher?

Once we begin thus to trace the many linkages that join these separate insights and build them into one insight, we begin to see that what psychologists and psychiatrists have collectively declared is that the business of man is to mature: to mature psychologically as well as physically, to mature along the line of what is unique in him and what he healthily shares with all his fellows, and to continue the maturing process throughout his life. This is the *maturity concept.* This is the concept that challenges us in the twentieth century, and that offers us hope.

TWO

CRITERIA OF MATURITY

THE HUMAN individual is not self-contained. His physical survival depends upon constant access to resources outside his body. In like manner, his growth into psychic individuality depends upon his having linked himself in one way or another with his environment.

The life that is psychologically poverty-stricken is one that has few such linkages—and these routine and noncreative. The life that is reactionary is one that has more linkages with the past than with the future. The life that is neurotic or psychotic is one that has linked itself to an environment not really there: its responses are to fantasies and illusions—to dangers that are the projections of its own fears; to slights that are the projections of its own self-doubtings. On the other hand, the life that is rich and happy is one that is fulfilling its possibilities through creative linkages with reality.

We can begin, then, to put meaning into the maturity concept. A mature person is not one who has come to a certain level of achievement and stopped there. He is rather a *maturing* person—one whose *linkages with life* are constantly becoming stronger and richer because his attitudes are such as to encourage their growth rather than their stoppage. A mature person, for example, is not one who knows a large number of facts. Rather, he is one whose mental habits are such that he grows in knowledge and in the wise use of it. A mature person is not one who has built up a certain quota of human relationships—family, friends, acquaintances, fellow workers—and is ready to call a halt, dismissing the rest of the human race as unimportant. Rather, he is a person who has learned how to operate well in a human environment so that he continues both to add new people to those whom he cares about and to discover new bases of fellowship with those already familiar.

When Diderot made his startling remark that all children are essentially criminal, he was saying, in effect, that human beings are safe to have around only if they are as weak in their powers of execution as they are in their powers of understanding. An infant with the strength and authority of a man would be a monster; for an infant has, as yet, established no linkages with life save those that minister to his own immediate desires.

He has no knowledge—therefore his acts of power would be also acts of ignorance. He has no mature affection, but mostly an ego-centered pleasure in those who give him what he wants—therefore his acts of power would aim solely at self-gratification. His imagination about other people is still a potential, not a realized power—therefore his acts of power would be acts of ruthlessness. He has no sense of the patience, skill, and labor that have gone into the construction of his environment—therefore his acts of power would, often, be acts of destruction. He has as yet no steadiness of character; no code of justice; no conviction about the meaning of life and of man's proper role—therefore his acts of power would be those of whim. In short, it is safe for a human being to grow in physical strength and self-determination only if he is building such linkages of knowledge and feeling that what he chooses to do is creative rather than destructive, social rather than antisocial.

By this standard, we might say that a person is properly maturing—whether he be five years old or fifty—only if his power over his environment is matched by a growing awareness of what is involved in what he does. If his powers of execution forge ahead while his powers of understanding lag behind, he is backward in his psychological growth—and dangerous to have around.

For precisely this reason, the most dangerous members of our society are those grownups whose powers of influence are adult but whose motives and responses are infantile. The adult has certain kinds of power denied to the infant. He has physical strength. If he still hits out at life with the anger of a frustrated infant, he can work more destruction and inflict more pain than would be possible to the person physically immature. In the second place, he has authority over someone: he is parent, teacher, employer, foreman, officer of a club, public official, or perhaps simply a member of a majority group that is permitted to keep members of a minority group "in their place." Few adults are without authority over anyone. The adult, therefore, whose emotional linkages with life are still undeveloped has a greater power to make other people miserable than has the child. In the third place, the adult has a vastly increased opportunity to add artificial to natural power through such devices as ownership and membership. He can drive a car and use its strength as his own; he can join an organization and use the influence of numerous others to press a cause he could not effectively press alone. If his linkages of knowledge and feeling are still as few and tenuous as those that fit the power-status of a five-year-old or even a ten-year-old, he can do harm beyond measure.

Discussing the reason why our human affairs are so fearfully out of joint, and applying to the problem his psychiatric experience, G. B. Chisholm has said, "So far in the history of the world there have never been enough mature people in the right places." Never yet, in short, have enough people come to their adulthood—and to adulthood's powers and prerogatives—with such sound linkages between them and their world that what they choose to do is for their own and the common good.

Briefly, then, we must explore some of the basic linkages with life that an individual must progressively establish if he is not merely to grow into adulthood but to become mature.

II

The human being is born ignorant. His body, to be sure, has certain kinds of "knowledge" that belong to it by nature. Even the newborn infant "knows," for example, how to make the sucking motions that enable it to take in food for survival. But in all super-instinctual matters the ignorance of that newborn infant is total. His world has, so far, told him virtually nothing about itself. He is ignorant not only of such specific cultural skills as reading, writing, and arithmetic— through which there may later be opened up to him well-nigh incredible vistas—but of even his own survival needs. He can register discomfort, but he cannot be said to know that he is uncomfortable because his blanket has slipped aside and left him cold. *He is at the total-ignorance level of a life in which the knowledge potential is enormous.*

He will never know all that he theoretically could know: it is part of our mortal fate that we die with powers yet unexpended. But he will not survive even his infancy unless he establishes some sort of *knowledge linkage* with his world. He will not mature psychologically unless that linkage is strong, and keeps growing stronger.

It would be folly for us to attempt to enumerate all the specific kinds of knowledge that a human being should acquire in order to rate as mature. One man of forty may know how to prune an orchard—and in that direction may act maturely through that knowledge. Another may know the ways of the stars in their courses; or how to treat the diseases of the human body; or how to load a truck so that there will be, in transit, no dangerous shifting of that load.

Of two men who walk side by side along a country lane only one may know the names and natures of the plants and trees they see; yet we will not on that account call the other man immature. We will not call him immature unless his attitude toward such knowledge brands him so. If his life work is such that he should, for effectiveness, know the names and natures of those plants and trees, but if he has chosen to bluff instead of to learn, then we can call him immature. We can call him so if he pretends to knowledge he does not possess. We can call him so, if, lacking a certain type of knowledge, he self-defensively holds that it is not worth possessing. We can call him so if this specific ignorance is but one expression of a kind of total obtuseness—a general indifference to the world he inhabits.

It is not, in brief, the mastery of this or that fact that marks a person as mature in his knowledge-relationship. It is, rather, his attitude toward knowing and the tie-up that exists between his knowledge and his situation.

If a person has no interest in any kind of knowledge except the sort that insures his animal survival, he is immature. He is leaving undeveloped whole areas of potentiality peculiar to his species. He is, moreover, almost guaranteeing that in many situations peculiarly human he will see too little and know too little to be wise and just in his responses.

If, again, a person, through his adult strength and status, exerts influence that calls for a certain kind of knowledge, and if he makes no effort to gain that knowledge, he is immature. In our culture, the adult is allowed to exert an influence upon his society through casting his ballot. If he makes no progressive effort to learn what is at stake in various issues before he throws the weight of his opinion and his vote on one side or another, he is immature. He is permitting his adult power to go unmatched by adult knowledge.

If, finally, a person takes it for granted that his present store of knowledge is sufficient for the rest of his life, he is immature. Not only will his responses to new situations be inadequate but his mind will develop rigidities of dogma and false pride that will make it into an unchanging anomaly in a changing world. In this respect, the unlettered farmer who does things as his father did them and has no use for "schoolbook agriculture" is neither more nor less immature in his attitude toward learning than is the classical scholar who has not changed an idea or a witticism through a generation of teaching.

Here, then, is one kind of linkage that the human being must progressively build with his world if he is to grow into mental, emotional, and social maturity. Where a person fails to build, and to go on building, the knowledge linkage, it may be, as Thorndike pointed out, partly for reasons within himself and partly for reasons outside himself. If a certain adult, for example, was once a child whose every show of interest in learning was squelched—perhaps by a father who taunted him with trying to rise above his family; or by a "religious" mother for whom education was synonymous with worldly pride; or by playmates who called him "teacher's pet" and shut him out of their games—that adult may well have within himself deep emotional reasons for leaving books alone. He may still, in his unconscious, be fighting out one of the major battles of his childhood; and he may be settling the issue as he finally tried to settle it in childhood—by adopting the standards of those around him in order to win a sense of belonging. Another adult who shows a similar lack of interest in learning may not have faced that particular problem. But all his life he has taken for granted the dogmas and rule of thumb practices of his family and neighborhood. He went through as much schooling as the other children of his group, with as much scorn of schooling and as little comprehension of it as the rest of them showed. He has, all his life, heard the same political, economic, and religious platitudes pronounced as ultimate truth—and to his ears they sound comfortably good. This individual, in brief, has, for reasons outside himself—reasons inherent in the mores—failed in his mental and emotional maturing. He meets adult situations— and therefore exerts his adult strength—with practically the same information and attitudes that he had when he was meeting childhood situations with childhood strength. Where new facts have been thrust upon his reluctant consciousness, he has quickly robbed them of their irritating quality by wrapping them up in a platitude and denying them any authority over his behavior. The potentialities of this person are as warped and wasted as are those of the person who has stopped learning for reasons inside himself, though his unconscious may be less scarred by battle. Both of these individuals—and their counterparts are legion—are immature in their adulthood; for they have cut short their maturing process and not tried to match increased powers with increased knowledge of what is at stake.

I I I

The human being is born irresponsible. He did not choose to enter the human scene; and for a long time after his entrance he is helpless to do much about it. Yet if we hear a grown man justify his lack of responsible participation in that scene by saying that, after all, he didn't ask to be born, we can set him down as immature. For one of the strong ties that must progressively link the individual to his world is that of responsibility; resentment against that fact, or inability to realize it in action, indicates a stoppage in psychological growth.

At the outset, there is nothing that the helpless infant can do for itself or for anyone else. Therefore it has a valid claim upon the attention of those who have brought it into being. In a very real sense, the world owes it a living.

Not many years pass, however, before the helpless infant grows into a child progressively capable of self-help and of help to others. It enters, in brief, upon the responsibility-life of man: there are things that it can do; there are things, therefore, that other people have a right to expect it to do as its share of the common enterprise. The toddler that fumblingly begins to learn how to dress itself is in training for emotional and social maturity. So is the growing boy who learns to go to the store on an errand and bring home what he went for. So is the adolescent who, driving the family car, shows due

respect for speed limits and for the hour when he has agreed
to return home. So, also, is the child or adolescent who learns
to stand out against the gang in behalf of a helpless animal
or an absent friend who is being "taken apart." So, often—
though parents may be reluctant to admit it—is the adolescent who tries out his own mind and his own budding idealism
by refusing meek conformity to the world as it is and to the
standards and rationalizations that his family and community
take for granted. Mature responsibility involves both a willing participation in the chores of life and a creative participation in the bettering of life. Year by year, as helplessness
turns into strength, the sound human being takes on a responsibility commensurate with his powers.

The responsibility linkage with life takes on maturity to
the extent that three conditions are being progressively fulfilled. In the first place, the individual has to learn to accept
his human role. When an adult pettishly protests that he
didn't ask to be born, he overlooks the simple fact that nobody else did either. Those whose services he commands had
as little to say about being born as he himself had. By his
standard, therefore, they have as much right as he to ask
that the world wait upon them—the only hitch being that
the people upon whom the world would have to depend are
also people who did not ask to be born. To mature, in brief,
is progressively to accept the fact that the human experience
is a shared experience; the human predicament, a shared
predicament. A person remains immature, whatever his age,
as long as he thinks of himself as an exception to the human
race.

The second condition of maturity involves the development of a sense of function. No one is mature except to the extent that there is work he accepts as his own, that he performs with a fair degree of expertness, and from which he draws a sense of significance. By this standard, a woman is immature if she wants all the advantages of marriage but resents the work she has to do to keep a home in running order and to bring up a family. Similarly, a man is immature if he regards the support of a family as a kind of trap in which he, an unsuspecting male, has somehow been caught. Again, the person who cannot settle down—who remains a vocational drifter; or the person who wants the prestige of a certain type of work but resents the routines that go with it, are immature in their sense of function.

The third condition of maturity involves the development of function-habits. A child does not yet know how to work out spheres of orderliness; he has as yet no accurate sense of time; he has no capacity to think through a complicated plan and to relate cause and effect so that he can predict what the results of his action will be; his attention-span is too brief to enable him to have constancy of purpose. In a very real sense, "A boy's will is the wind's will." Unfortunately, however, a good many grownups, without any such legitimate reason, are as veering and unstable as children.

Some of these adults can best be described as *distracted*, the classic parody of them being the White Queen in *Through a Looking Glass:* a poor bedazed woman, always on the run, whose hair refused to hold its pins, whose shawl would not stay straight because it was "out of temper," and whose words, like the mind behind them, went in all directions at once and arrived nowhere. Such people *know* that life is out of hand; they are forever frantic with their efforts to master it; but the things they do are never serenely part of an over-all plan.

Other adults who lack the habits with which to carry on a mature function can be described as *bumbling*. They expend enough energy, patience, and good intention; but they seem so to lack a sense of cause and effect that they are always miserably discovering that they have done the wrong thing. Yet others are *self-excusing*. Though they may habitually be late for their appointments, for example, there is always a slow clock to blame, or a traffic congestion, or a friend who *would* keep them talking. Others are *self-dramatizing*. They enjoy the image of themselves as unconventional, as showing a certain touch of genius in their difference from the common run of men.

The journey from irresponsibility to responsibility is full of hazards. Every individual first encounters his problems of security and personal significance while he is still a helpless infant. His first efforts to get what he wants are made long before he enjoys either independence or competence. They are, therefore, directed at getting other people to give him what he wants. Thus, at the most vulnerable time of his life, he faces a double danger: of consolidating habits of "successful" dependence upon others, so that he never finds a sufficient motive for growing into mature responsibility; or of experiencing so much frustration that his natural drive toward independence is replaced either by a submissive acceptance of whatever happens or by an aggressive resistance.

We now know that many irresponsible adult behaviors stem from causes other than their apparent causes. The person who is never on time, for example, even though he consciously tries for punctuality, may be expressing an unconscious resentment carried over from childhood: resentment, perhaps, against stringent rules of "niceness" and orderliness that set him apart from his playmates and won him the label of sissy. The bumbling person who seems pitifully to fail, and fail again, in spite of honest effort, may unconsciously want to fail—because failure allows him to remain in some measure dependent.

Man, in brief, does not grow automatically from dependence to independence, helplessness to competence, irresponsibility to responsibility. But the linkage with life brought about by such growth is indispensable to maturity.

IV

The human being is born inarticulate. In a peculiar sense he is born alone. As he matures, he will build word-linkages between himself and his world.

Most children soon learn to talk the language of the people around them. Yet few of them continue their verbal maturing throughout life. Few of them, in adulthood, are so able to say what they want to say—with confidence, precision, beauty, and a sensitive awareness of what is fitting in the situation—that the communicative experience holds more of success than of failure. In no area of our maturing, in fact, is arrested development more common than in the area of communication. It is so common that it is not even noticed; it is taken for granted as natural. The person who is mature in his communicative powers is noted as an exception to the rule. The person who is immature—halting, clumsy, obscure, rambling, dull, platitudinous, insensitive—is the rule.

Here, once more, we must look to the environment of the infant and the growing child for the causes. Three factors seem largely to account for arrested development in the area of speech.

The first factor is a simple one: unless some unusual influence enters to change the pattern, most children grow up talking as the adults around them talk. If the speech they hear from their first moment of consciousness is undistinguished and banal, their own is likely to become so. If the speech they hear is fretful with irritation and self-pity; or is an instrument of malice; or is loaded with dogmatism and prejudice, their own is likely to be so. Mediocrity is marvelously transmissible by contagion, and never more so than in the area of speech.

The second factor involves the child's first efforts to communicate and the reception accorded those efforts. The small human being who tries, desperately sometimes, to communicate a need through pre-language sounds or through half-formed words cannot be expected to realize that the people whom he is trying to reach cannot catch his meaning: that even with the best of intentions, they have to guess; and that often they will guess wrong. Every person, it seems safe to say, experiences a good many angers and frustrations in the area of speech before he escapes the initial inarticulateness to which he is born. Where the environment is one of unmistakable love, these angers and frustrations may have small lasting consequence. But where the environment is one of indifference, impatience, or actual hostility, they may become part of a pervasive, unconscious insecurity, and expectation of failure.

Even after the child has grown into a fair articulateness, his efforts to communicate may be so received that the process of his verbal maturing is discouraged and brought to an eventual halt. This may happen if he is teased and taunted for the way he talks; or if he is constantly out-talked by big-voiced adults and older brothers and sisters; or if the people around him are habitually too busy or self-absorbed to give him more than an absent-minded flick of attention, so that he repeatedly finds himself talking in a psychological vacuum; or if the private feelings he has confided are made public as something to laugh about. The halting of his growth may result, on the other hand, from a too easy success. If "baby talk" that is continued far into childhood is praised as cute; if he is constantly invited to show off; if the whole adult world seems to stop and lend a concerned ear whenever he speaks, unriddling every fumbling word and satisfying every need almost before it is expressed, the motive for the building of the word-linkage with life may be too weak to be effective. Why go through the hard labor of learning to talk well if one can be the center of the universe without that labor?

The third factor is only indirectly related to the child's actual speech experience. To understand it we have to realize that our verbal linkage with life is not merely a word-linkage, it is a character linkage *through* words. Speech defects not caused by actual organic malformation are understood, most often, as character defects, as an expression of some basic failure to work out a right relationship with life. Stammerings, stutterings—these and other speech difficulties are now widely recognized as having their roots in emotional disturbances: in irrational fears, guilt feelings, hostilities. But such "speech defects" as habitual dullness, pomposity, sarcasm, nagging, whining, monologuing, irrelevant meandering, oversweetness, lack of tact, platitudinizing, pedantry, and a meticulous, indiscriminate stressing of details to the disadvantage of over-all significance—these, too, should properly be regarded as "character defects"; as evidence that the individual has, for some reason inherent in his emotional experience, failed to continue his psychological growth.

Because speech defects in this broader sense are so common among us they are scarcely noticed. They attract no more attention than a cripple would in a community of cripples.

When we begin to understand the role that speech plays in life, we cannot dismiss the prevalent immaturity of speech. Speech is that through which we most constantly influence one another. From the words of a mother to her child to the words of one diplomat to another, speech is a maker of psychological universes. Speech, again, is that through which we most commonly seek to escape our skin-enclosed isolation and to enter into a community of experience. Again, it is that through which we clarify our ideas and beliefs: putting these out into the public medium of language, we discover whether or not they make sense. Furthermore, it is that through which we transmit knowledge and experience: acting out our human role as builders of a tradition. Finally, speech is man's most ready emotional safety valve. Tests relative to the joys, fears, and angers of different age groups have established the fact, for example, that whereas children of the eight- and nine-year-old group tend to express strong emotion through physical action, adolescents and adults tend to express it through words. For the most part, however, the type of release they are able to enjoy is woefully inadequate, because they have grown to the age of verbal release of tension without growing verbally mature. They are unable to do more than stutter with emotion; or brood themselves into explosive anger. They are bound, likewise, by the sheer paucity of the words at their command; they can do nothing more than repeat the expletives, clichés, and slang phrases that have already been worn meaningless with use, so that they never have a chance, through words, to express the strong uniqueness of their own human experience.

We may, then, set this down as another basic fact about ourselves: our lives are in good order only if the communicative linkages between us and our world are relatively mature and becoming more so.

V

The human being is born a creature of diffuse sexuality. He must mature toward a specific and creative sexual relationship.

Through the studies of psychologists and psychiatrists, we have already, during this century, taken long strides toward an understanding of our sex nature; but we still have far to go before a full and happy maturing of that nature will be our common lot. Sexual immaturity of one sort and another is still—like communicative immaturity—so prevalent as to seem normal.

Certain facts about our sex nature and development are now clear. The first of these is that our sexuality is born with us; it does not mysteriously come into our lives at some later date. At first it is, apparently, little more than a diffuse potential. But it is there from the beginning and colors our earliest strongly felt relationships to other people: to our parents, first of all. Sexual jealousies and attachments are part of the emotional experience of even very young children; and if they are misunderstood or mishandled, they become the source of self-doubtings, guilt feelings, and hostilities which, lodged in the unconscious, may distort all later relationships.

A second fact is that our sex nature goes through certain normal stages of development before it reaches its maturity. Because of some emotional experience, it may be arrested at any one of these stages. It is almost common knowledge, now—though still pushed off by some people as not "nice"— that small children go through a period of possessive attachment to the parent of the opposite sex. The small toddling girl, only recently emerged from infancy and ill-equipped as yet to handle any emotional problems, "falls in love" with her father, wants him to belong wholly to her, and resents her mother's claim upon him. The small boy similarly attaches himself to his mother. This first period of heterosexual experience is, we have come to realize, the source of many unresolved conflicts that later make their home in the unconscious. It is a wrenching period, not because of what the child feels, but because he does not know how to fit his intense feelings into the context of his life. He is dependent upon both parents; supposed to love both. Resenting one of them—even wishing for the death of that one—he is torn by both fear and guilt: the security-pattern of his life is threatened; but he cannot acknowledge what he actually feels.

This story has been told so often, now, in psychiatric literature, that it is almost an old story. Yet most parents still either remain unaware of the child's inner conflict or greet the outward manifestations of it so as to intensify that conflict. If parents are dependable in their affection for the child; if they do not let themselves become upset by his sudden bursts of hostility; if they give him as much chance as possible to be significant in his own right; and if they are so steadily and deeply attached to each other that the child soon realizes the uselessness of trying to divide them, there is every likelihood that, after a brief period of turmoil, his progress toward sexual maturity will resume its healthy course. If, on the other hand, the beloved parent is either indifferent or overindulgent, while the other parent is hurt or jealous; if they compete for the child's affection; or if they are so at odds with each other that he is almost driven to take sides, there is a sad likelihood that a residual immaturity will mark the individual's sex relationships all through his life.

Other stages of sexual development follow in their natural course and bring their own dangers. Growing children go through a period of normal "homosexuality": girls like girls, at this stage, and dislike boys; boys like boys, and have no patience with the curls and foibles of girlhood. If they arrive at this stage with their earlier heterosexual problems well out of the way, they are not likely to become fixated in a permanent homosexuality. But if they are already carrying a burden of unresolved guilt, it may happen that they will head toward an adulthood of psychological, if not physical, homosexuality. The girl may grow up into a woman who still feels that all men are crude and filthy-minded; the boy into a man who still despises women and is happiest as part of a male gang.

Adolescence is the second period of intense heterosexuality. Now, however, the object of affection is not the parent of opposite sex, but a member of the young person's own age group. There are several reasons why adolescence is a problem-time. Glandular and other bodily changes are taking place with distracting rapidity and are accompanied by such mental and emotional changes that the individual hardly knows himself. Also, at least in our culture, it is a period when the boy or girl, on the verge of adulthood, is needing to feel independent and is in frequent conflict with parental standards. Since intensified sexual feelings and an intensified need to prove himself as an individual are coincidental, they tend to merge—and a flouting of sex standards becomes one of the preferred ways of establishing independence. Relationships to members of the opposite sex in most cases are not steady. The individual falls into love and out of love. Other factors not themselves sexual may add to the adolescent's emotional unrest and may color his attitude toward sex, such as uneasiness about his vocational future, or constant awareness that he may be caught in war before he can build a life of his own. Many conflicts, in brief, heighten the sexual tensions of adolescence and may, if unresolved, encourage a lasting immaturity. The philanderer, for example, who all his life drifts from one woman to another, is a person whose sexual maturing has been arrested at the adolescent level. No one can be called sexually mature, it would seem, until he accepts his own sex nature without guilt; incorporates that nature in a rational life-plan; and is able to make sexual experience the basis of a sustained, mutually fulfilling, and creative relationship with the opposite sex.

A third fact regarding our sexual behaviors is only beginning to penetrate. This is the fact that sexual behaviors do not rise far above or fall far below the level of our nonsexual behaviors. Sex is one channel through which we express our character. It is not a thing apart from that character. We do not find, for example, that a person whose sexual behavior is marked by a will to dominate and exploit others is a person who, in other areas of his life, has a mature gift for equality. Nor do we find that the person who regards sex as filthy has, in other respects, a finely rational power to measure the worth of things. Psychiatrists are revising some of their first estimates regarding the role of sex. They are beginning to note that while it remains true that a traumatic sex experience can so arrest development that an individual's whole relationship to life will be distorted, it is equally true that a traumatic experience in some other area of life will have a similar effect and will, in part, express itself through the channel of sexual behavior.

We are still far from having the full-rounded knowledge of our human nature out of which sexual maturity can confidently grow. But we are at least at the point where we can state with assurance that where the sex linkage is immature there is no high maturity of character.

VI

The human being is born self-centered. To be sure, he has as yet no clearly defined "self" in which to center. But even less does he have any power to relate himself to other selves. One of the most important phases of maturing is that of growth from self-centering to an understanding relationship to others; from egocentricity to sociocentricity. A person is not mature until he has both an ability and a willingness to see himself as one among others and to do unto those others as he would have them do to him.

The very existence of a society implies certain forces that temper the raw egocentricity of the newborn; for without such tempering, there cannot be mutual support, common purposes, structured reliance of man upon man. Parents, other adults, older children, and soon other children of the same age group all exert an influence that encourages the child to relate himself to persons other than himself. Smiles and frowns are ways of inducting him into the delights and perils of a social world. Early in life he is taught not to grab everything for himself, not to make a howling nuisance of himself. He is taught to enter happily into the group business of making plans and of realizing those plans. He is taught that there are rules so binding that his own stubborn will cannot flout them with impunity.

In brief, so far as the little self-contained ego is concerned, growing up means growing *into*—growing into a complex set of social relationships: linkages of affection, sympathy, shared work, shared beliefs, shared memories, good will toward fellow humans.

The human potential that seems to be chiefly involved in this phase of man's maturing is *imagination*. Imagination is defined as a "mental synthesis of new ideas from elements experienced separately." It is not, as is so often thought, a process of making something out of nothing. Imagination is rather a process of making *new wholes* out of *familiar parts*.

From the moment of birth the infant has things happen to him that give him feelings of well-being or ill-being. These are direct and immediate experiences. At first he knows them only as his own. He has no equipment of imagination for realizing that a pin-prick which makes him cry with pain will cause similar pain to another person. As he matures, however, he develops an increasing power to make mental syntheses "of new ideas from elements experienced separately." He is able to turn *his* experience into *human* experience. He grows, in brief, in social imagination. If he continues thus to grow, his adult strength will be a blessing to those around him, not a curse. For every additional power that he has taken on will have been matched by an additional sensitivity to what it means to be human. He will do unto others as he would have them do unto him because he will feel their feelings as he does his own.

Psychologists are giving currency to a word that is useful in this connection: *empathy*, which signifies the imaginative projection of one's own consciousness into an object or person outside oneself. We sympathize with another being when we suffer *with* him; when we feel *with* him. But an empathic relationship is closer: we then enter imaginatively *into* his life and feel it as if it were our own. Though our bodily separateness remains, we effect a psychic identification. We stop being an outsider and become an insider.

Most people have more empathic experiences than they realize. If they notice them at all, they give them only a passing attention and do not bother to ask through what power they have briefly but vividly entered into another person's being—thus triumphing, as it were, over isolation. At a track meet, for example, virtually all the members of a watching crowd will "help" the pole vaulter to clear the high bar. In a very real psychological sense, they rise with him as he vaults; they share his muscular strain; they enter into the moment of suspense; they descend with him in defeat or triumph—and most of them never give more than a flick of thought, if they give that much, to the psychic mystery of their experience. Similarly, most people will enter into any acute embarrassment that is suffered by a person in their presence—unless some emotional block prevents their doing so. They do not merely sympathize with the humiliated person; they "borrow" his humiliation, and feel it within themselves. Our everyday experience, in brief, testifies to the fact that empathy is one of our human potentials and that it can go far toward saving man from psychic isolation. Also, however, our everyday experience, and the desperate plight of our world, testify to the fact that the empathic potential remains chiefly a potential. Those whom it has genuinely released from immature egocentricity into mature sociocentricity are rare among us. The arrested development of the imagination is, perhaps, the most common tragedy of our human existence.

Doubtless there are many reasons for the early arrest of this power in us; but three such reasons seem to be of prime importance.

The first is obvious: a vast number of children receive their first influence from parents who are themselves emotionally and socially immature. Such parents confirm the child in his egocentricity instead of helping him to outgrow it. They may do so by making him so insecure that he is almost forced into a concentrated self-absorption: by neglecting him; teasing him; comparing him unfavorably with other children; quarreling over him; ridiculing him for mistakes that are, as often as not, the product of an overanxious effort to please; visiting upon him moods generated by adult worries but never so explained to him. They may, again, keep him egocentric by rewarding egocentricity: by yielding to his every whim; by making him the one fixed center of the domestic universe; by urging him, constantly, to hold his own against other children rather than to share with them.

The second reason is less obvious. In most homes, schools, communities, and even churches, children are encouraged to achieve only a limited or provincial growth beyond egocentricity. They are supposed to become properly socio-centered in their relationships to special people and special groups of people—family, friends, members of the same class, race, religion, and nation—but they are discouraged from extending their empathic imagination to include "outsiders." We said earlier that a person will, in some measure, enter into the acute embarrassment of another person—unless some emotional block prevents his doing so. Here we discover, perhaps, the nature of the most common emotional block: the habit of *empathic provincialism.* Many people who would suffer the humiliation of a friend, or even of a stranger who belonged to their own class or race, as though it were their own, will remain indifferent to the humiliation of a member of a different class or race. They are quite literally unable to believe that this "outsider" actually has the same feelings that they and their kind experience. It is this type of provincial imagination that accounts for the perennial capacity of many people to be kind within the family circle and yet indifferent to sufferings of people outside that circle; to be strictly honest in dealing with members of their own class and yet shrewd and ruthless to the point of dishonesty when they extend their influence across class lines.

The third reason is to be found in the fact that most people within our culture are encouraged to live by contradictory sets of values: they are urged to be both *for* other people as human brothers and *against* them as competitors; to be unselfish yet to look, first of all, after themselves. This is to say that they are both encouraged to develop the power of empathy and discouraged from developing it. The not astonishing result is that human relationships among us are more confused than clear—and that many confusions that exist within individuals are projected upon others in the form of hostility.

The overshadowing tragedy of our human existence is that so vast a number of people grow into adulthood with their social imagination arrested. They take on the powers of adulthood, but they are incapable of feeling what happens to other people or of greatly caring whether those others fare well or ill.

VII

The human being is born to a world of isolated particulars. He has to mature into a world of wholes.

At first, he has only *this* pain; *this* satisfaction; *this* fear; *this* anger—all of them tied together by some vague sense of identity. When William James spoke of the first experience of the infant as a big, buzzing confusion, he may have assumed too much knowledge in an area into which no grown-up mind can really enter; yet it seems fair to assume that the newborn child has as yet no experience of *wholeness*—that is, of parts significantly related to one another; of many parts making a total from which each separate part draws meaning. It is in the direction of *whole*-seeing and *whole*-thinking that growth must take place if maturity is ever to be achieved. However much of a "buzzing confusion" the infant may experience at first, the time soon comes when his crib, his room, his toys, the people who come and go, who lift him up and put him down and feed him when he is hungry, take on a certain coherence. Things begin to hang together. The child begins to learn what follows from what. Out of heterogeneous data, he begins to build coherent expectations.

As he grows, the areas in which things hang together become larger and more complex: not merely his crib but the whole house becomes his province; then the street; school; buses; stores; the whole city; other cities; the place where he works; the associations to which he belongs; the girl he marries and the home he creates; the newspaper he reads and the various forms of entertainment he enjoys; the nation; the human race. What was at first a pin-point world takes on size; what was at first a purely physical world takes on a dimension of abstraction—of generalization; principle. What was at first a world of immediacy becomes a world with past and future.

Life, in short, is a process of entering into—as well as creating—*wholes of meaning.* In a quite literal sense, the child-mind sees in part and prophesies in part. When that which is whole is come, that which is in part is not so much "done away" as it is lifted up into its full significance. As we develop the power thus to lift up the part into the whole, our linkage to life becomes *philosophical.* Whether an individual acts as businessman, farmer, mechanic, educator, diplomat, parent, voter, employer, or what not, he is philosophical—and to that extent mature—in the degree that he sees *whole* and prophesies *whole;* in the degree, that is, that he takes into account *all* that is involved in a situation and ties to that "all" both his present behaviors and his future plans and expectations.

Situations beyond number are distorted by the influence of full-grown men and women who still "see in part and prophesy in part." They see with the eyes of their own little, limited world, their own wishes, prides, moods, preoccupations, irritations, ignorances, prejudices, privileges, ambitions, and conditionings. And on the basis of what they thus see, they "prophesy." That is, they act in terms of cause-and-effect linkages that are as faulty and restricted as their seeing. The teacher who carries into the classroom a personal anger and takes it out on the children, sees in the situation only what her anger bids her see. She does not see what she is doing to the children and to her own relationship with them through a long chain of tomorrows. The politician who goes to the state legislature or the national Congress to promote the cause of the particular pressure group that has elevated him to office sees in part and prophesies in part: he has no eye for the welfare of the whole society and he does not begin to glimpse the long range consequences of what he does. Intent to please those who have pleased him, he is able to prophesy his own re-election; but he is too short-sighted to prophesy, for example, the squandering of natural resources that may result from his helping his particular pressure group to operate with a free hand.

Plato saw slight hope for human society until such time as philosophers should be made kings. G. B. Chisholm was speaking in the Platonic vein when he said that never yet in the history of the world have there been enough mature people in the right places. He was speaking in the Platonic vein; but he was going further than Plato went. Being a psychiatrist, with a psychiatrist's knowledge of how human beings are shaped in their character structures by a myriad different influences, he would not be satisfied to have philosophers merely in the role of kings. He would know that the "right places" for philosophers—for people who have a mature power to see *whole*—are all those places where influence extends from one individual to another. He would know—as more and more of us are beginning to learn—that in this world of intricate mutual relationships no person is safe to have around if he has grown to his adulthood without building a fairly sound philosophical linkage with his world.

VIII

This chapter suggests, and the rest of the book will try to develop, what we shall call the *linkage theory of maturity*. This theory sees man as a creature who lives by and through relationships: who becomes himself through linkages with the nonself. It sees him, as a unit of psychic experience, both capable of lifelong growth and subject to arrest of growth at any point where he habitually makes immature efforts at problem-solving.

In this chapter, we have indicated certain linkages so basic to our human growth that if they remain unformed or ill-formed, we remain fixated in our mental, emotional, and social development: linkages of knowledge, responsibility, communication, mature sexuality, empathy, and philosophy. The fact that these have been separately and successively listed must not be interpreted to mean that they are independent of one another. The linkage theory of maturity is one of constellated powers or functions. It sees the individual, not as finely mature in one phase of his being and woefully immature in another, but as possessed of a *character structure* in which the several maturities or immaturities are closely related to one another.

This way of considering the individual as a whole of interdependent powers goes counter to prevalent habits of thought. We have liked to believe that a person can be ruthless in his business dealings and yet be a "good husband and father"; or that, because of his good intentions, he can be a first-rate citizen without knowing the actual facts involved in any issue. We have defended our illusions in this respect by making the definitions of "success" and "goodness" so narrow that even fairly flagrant immaturity can qualify. Thus, by ordinary standards, a man is a vocational success if he "earns a good living"; if he climbs "to the top of the ladder." He may achieve his "success" by means that do profound hurt to other people: by selling shoddy goods; publishing a newspaper that stirs up racial hatreds; giving such concentrated attention to money-making that his personal relationships are neglected and distorted. But he will not commonly be called a failure unless he loses his position or wealth. By similarly naïve standards, a woman may be called a good mother if she keeps her children well dressed and well fed, gives them various educational and social advantages, and marries them off well —even though, because of her influence, they carry into their adulthood sexual pruderies that they call high ideals or social snobbishnesses that make them incapable of liking anyone not markedly prosperous. Or, once more, a person may be accepted as successful in communication simply because he has a large vocabulary and an adroit capacity for holding the center of the stage, even though what he says is far more ego-centered than socio-centered; far more expressive of arrogance than of empathy.

For our human salvation, we must rid ourselves of such illusions as have made us accept immaturity as maturity. Reluctant as we may be to do so, we must acknowledge the hard fact that "to him that hath shall be given; and from him that hath not, even that which he hath shall be taken away." Because of the interdependence of our powers, maturity in one area of our life promotes maturity in other areas; immaturity in one area promotes immaturities in other areas. In fact, the human individual is a fairly tight-knit pattern of consistency. If, for example, he is markedly ego-centered, we can infallibly predict that he will not be highly mature in his responsibility linkages; or in his sexual life; or in his power to see things whole. If, on the other hand, he is markedly socio-centered, we can predict that his sense of responsibility will be keen; his sexual life will be marked by mature considerateness; and his power to see all that is involved in a situation will be highly developed.

This, then, is the first basic fact about the linkage theory of maturity: it does not measure psychological maturity by any single, isolated trait in a person, but by a constellation of traits—by a total character structure.

IX

A second basic fact about the linkage theory must also be noted: it does not make maturity synonymous with *adjustment*. While it recognizes that an immature person who is also "unadjusted" is in a miserable state and needs help, it recognizes no less that, given certain cultural conditions, the immature person is likely to effect a smoother "adjustment" than is the mature person. He is not, however, because he can adjust himself, on that account a more genuinely fulfilled person. Nor is his influence any less disastrous: his immaturities may be so like the accepted immaturities of the people around him that he and they will move in remarkable harmony; but his immaturity and theirs will continue to create situations in which human powers are frustrated. The standards they set will reward grown men and women for acting like children: ignorantly, irresponsibly, egocentrically, and so on. Christ, Roger Bacon, Abraham Lincoln, and many others like them, were all out of adjustment with the going attitudes and practices of their times; but they could hardly be regarded, on that account, as having been immature.

The linkage theory, in brief, declares that it is no longer safe or sufficient to judge the immaturities and maturities of men by the average practices of any institutions or any total culture. Rather, institutions and cultures must be judged by the extent to which they encourage or discourage maturity in all their members. The Sabbath, we have been told, was made for man; not man for the Sabbath. Homes, schools, churches, political parties, economic and social institutions, nations—these are made for man; not man for them. Human nature arrived on the scene first. The test of any institution is the releasing service it renders to that nature. As we explore the problem of maturity, then, we shall not be talking either as if the individual existed in a vacuum or as if he existed in an environment of institutions and customs so much more important than his little self that his highest duty and happiness was to "adjust." Holding in mind the kinds of linkage that are essential to human fulfillment, we shall lay a psychological measuring rod against both individual behaviors and social institutions; and we shall affirm, as man's unalienable right, the right to grow in an environment conducive to growth.

THREE

TWO OLD THEORIES AND
A NEW ONE

THROUGHOUT the pre-psychological ages, two theories about human misbehavior prevailed. Even in our present psychological age, the influence of these two theories continues to be largely undisputed. They determine the things we do to encourage desirable and to discourage undesirable behavior.

The first of these is the goodness-badness theory. People do good—so the theory holds—because there is good in them; they do evil because there is evil in them. The business of life is to persuade—or compel—people to stop being bad; and to persuade—or compel—them to be good. This theory has been most strongly held by believers in an authoritarian code, who conceive the task at home, church, school, and organized society as that of discouraging native tendencies to "badness" and of encouraging tendencies to "goodness" or "virtue." This theory has had a strong appeal for the ordinary person in authority—parent, teacher, employer, policeman, prison warden, public official. Unless a person is himself unusually mature, his first quick response to any offending behavior that makes extra work for him, or that makes him look foolish, or that disturbs the orderly arrangement of things, is to think of it in terms of its effect upon him and to call the offender a "bad" person.

The psychologist and the psychiatrist do not thus see the offender as a "bad" person. They tend to see him, rather, as a person in some way out of gear with life—who strikes out at life, as a child does in his angry frustration. No one, they realize, is knowingly evil. No one just up and says, "I'm bad, and I intend to be bad." Or if he does, the words tell less about moral evil in him than they do about frustration. They tell that the individual has, in his effort to gain attention, come to some point of desperation where he would rather be noticed for wrong-doing, and even be punished for it, than not be noticed at all. By and large, every so-called bad person has an excuse for himself that is, from his point of view, a perfectly good one: "Everybody's getting his. Why shouldn't I?" . . . "He did me dirt. That's why I bumped him off." Or, more subtly, he believes that what other people call bad is really good. Poor reasoning, all this, perhaps; but reasoning nevertheless—reasoning dictated by deep emotional needs; often by unconscious emotional needs. Because it is reasoning —however poor—it shows the misbehaving individual to have, not an unadulterated *will-to-evil*, but a circumscribed and fumbling mind.

The second traditional theory is the knowledge-ignorance theory. This has been the beloved of schools, colleges, and universities. It has, in general, derived less support from the authoritarian and far more from the liberal mind than has the goodness-badness theory; for a belief in it implies a confidence that the human being has powers which, if they are properly developed, will make him see what is right and therefore naturally impel him to do what is right. Even Socrates, seeing the mischievous effects of ignorance—particularly of self-ignorance—was bold to declare that knowledge is virtue; and every teacher who has sought to gain self-respect through his calling has echoed the Socratic words. To dispel ignorance, to bring people to an awareness of the facts of their world, to get them to know the truth about things and people, events and relations—this has seemed a sublime undertaking. We might say that most schools, colleges, and universities carry above their portals the invisible legend, "Seek ye first the kingdom of knowledge and all the rest will be added unto you."

As in the case of the goodness-badness theory, this view has had the support of a widespread folk-conviction. This has been particularly true in America, where one chief expression of social optimism has taken the form of a belief in the inexhaustible powers of factual knowledge. By and large, Americans have had an enormous faith in education—even when they have not defined it. Through this faith they have expressed both their feeling that things are sure to become better, and their generous feeling that most people are a pretty good lot. Even though they may, in their moments of anger, or in their area of authority, act out the goodness-badness theory, they tend in their more relaxed moments, and in their appraisal of life in general, to feel that if only enough people can be enough educated in the knowledge of the what, why, and how of things, all will be right with the world.

The adventure of searching out facts has been a noble one. The devoted efforts of knowledge-seekers to fill minds with facts have been of tremendous importance. Yet when we regard the curious perversities to be found among many "educated" adults—self-absorptions, pettinesses, fears, ego-tisms, prejudices, dogmatisms, pedantries—we are forced to wonder whether the dispelling of ignorance is anything more than the merest beginning of wisdom, not its achievement.

The psychologist and psychiatrist take issue with the knowledge-ignorance account of human misbehavior, as they do with the goodness-badness account. This is not to say that they hold factual knowledge to be unimportant. On the contrary, as we have already suggested, the knowledge linkage with life is one of the basic linkages developed in the matur-ing process. But these modern investigators of our human make-up differ from the traditional educator and the ra-tionalistic philosopher on two counts: they attach a dif-ferent type of importance to the possession of knowledge; and they see different limits to what knowledge can accom-plish. They are certain that knowledge is not *by itself* enough to redeem life from bewilderment and folly. It is enough only in constellation with other powers.

For one thing, the function of knowledge is not merely to

help the individual solve a specific problem. It is, rather, to help him gain an increased self-confidence through the experience of solving problems correctly—a self-confidence that frees him from the necessity of resorting to immature and disguised methods of proving his own significance.

To take a case in point, the old-line educator could not imagine that it might be an actual misfortune for a boy to be a "good student" and to get "good grades." The psychiatrist, on the other hand, might easily conceive of such a situation—one, for example, in which a student's bookish concentration expressed, not a free and productive love of what he was studying, but a driving need to outdo others; or an inability to enter into social relationships with others; or a constant fear of punishment if his grades should fall below a standard set by a demanding father. What such a student might gain by having the facts at his command would be far outweighed by the disruptive emotions associated with his experience of gaining such facts.

For another thing, the power of facts to influence a life is limited, as the psychiatrist sees it, by the individual's capacity to accept those facts even after he has "learned" them. They may theoretically exist in his mind without existing in his character structure. Just as an infant may be unable to assimilate food, not because the food is unpalatable, nor because of an organic illness, but because of an emotional disturbance, so the person of any age may be unable to assimilate facts.

We might recall here, by way of analogy, the case of a small boy who was losing weight and had no appetite. Nothing that he ate, under parental urging, seemed to agree with him. The family doctor could find no organic reason for his trouble. In the psychological clinic, however, to which he was eventually taken, an emotional reason was gradually brought to light. The child was in a state of deep rebellion against his mother's perfectionistic demands upon him and her strict insistence that he be, at all times and in all detailed respects, "a credit to the family." Because the hazards of open rebellion were too great to face, and also because his need to defy his mother and establish his own ego-identity was irresistible, the child was doing indirectly—and unconsciously—what he could not do directly. He was "refusing" the food his mother urged upon him—food that had become to him the symbol of her power over him. We recognize that his behavior was childish: that he was seeing in part and prophesying in part; for his method of building up his own ego took into account only a fragment of a total situation and, moreover, could be carried through to its logical conclusion only by his own defeat through death.

When we say, however, that his method was childish, we are not saying that he was a *bad* boy to employ that method. We are saying that the resources he had at his command for the solving of a deeply disturbing problem were so inadequate that they could not possibly accomplish the ends he had in view. For his "own good," he should have eaten his regular three meals a day; yet for his "own good," *as he felt that good*, he had to reject those meals. In similar fashion, people of all ages are driven to reject facts that, by all obvious standards, would be for their own good. They reject those facts, not simply with their minds but with their total make-up, because the acceptance of them would mean giving up something that now supports or magnifies their ego. Where personal worth is soundly based, it does not have to be on the defensive against facts. But where an adult is still getting his sense of significance out of immature relationships with his world, he has to defend himself against facts that would destroy that significance. From the psychiatric point of view, then, knowledge can become virtue only if it enters into an emotional context that makes its assimilation possible.

II

It seems clear, then, that neither the goodness-badness nor the knowledge-ignorance theory is adequate. In their stead we must place the maturity-immaturity theory. Increasingly we must see that human misbehaviors are *immature ways of solving problems that should be solved in ways that are mature.*

Though not always so labeled, this maturity-immaturity theory has already become so much a part of our thinking that it has passed into the institutional news of our time. Every day's newspaper brings us an account of some kind of "adjustment program," "guidance clinic," "counseling service," "parent education program," "mental hygiene program." In no one of these is the goodness-badness theory in evidence —for in no one of them is the human being thought of as an evil person who must be preached or chastised into goodness. Again, in no one of them is the knowledge-ignorance theory in evidence—for in no one of them is there exclusive provision for "instruction." On the contrary, in every one of them the thought prevails that individuals get variously caught in the meshes of life and have to be variously helped to find their way out. In all these programs, the person in trouble is assumed to be in difficulty because he is somehow out of gear with life; and the working theory of them all is that such a person needs, neither preachment nor mere facts, but a new character orientation toward his world.

This need for a total orientation is becoming so clear in the area of sex education—to take one example—that many well-intentioned parents and teachers are left in some bewilderment as to what they must do. In an awakened concern, some years ago, about the sex problems of young people, many high schools and colleges instituted courses on sex education. Almost exclusively, at first, the aim was to teach "facts about sex." However, as time has gone on and experience has accumulated, a new insight has begun to prevail. Thus Dr. Benjamin Gruenberg writes, "The behavior of the child or the adult—specifically, here, the sex behavior—is not in any significant degree the result of the formal or informal instruction he has received . . . 'sex education is an integral part of character and personality education'—*not a subject of instruction.*"

In other words, rescuing people from *sex ignorance* is far from enough. "So long as people generally," he continues, "assumed that human behavior was chiefly a matter of correct ideas, good intentions, and voluntary conformity, deviations from the sex-social conventions could be treated as specific failures or wilfulnesses." [1] With a deepened awareness of the character disturbances that may prevent a normal maturing of the individual, we can no longer be satisfied to treat sexual deviations as specific failures to be remedied by specific admonition or instruction. We begin to realize, instead, that they must be treated as part of a larger context of character. Only as the total character matures will sex problems reach a mature solution.

What is true in the area of sex education is true also in other areas. All along the line, in fact, we are beginning to act out a new insight: namely, that each person is a *whole* person and that it will be in his wholeness that he will reveal such fixations and emotional disturbances as keep him immature.

This insight is already operative, for example, on the pioneering edge of personnel work. While in many firms, what is called personnel work is still nothing more than an effort to make employees satisfied to do what their employers want them to do, in many other firms such work represents an honest effort to understand employees *as whole people*. Where this is true, a man's behavior on the job is not treated as though it were a specific something that could be isolated from all his other behaviors. It is treated as revealing his over-all relationship to life. Thus if a worker is habitually self-defensive, or belligerent, or overeager to please, or sulky, or subject to irrational angers, or self-pityingly convinced that everyone who is promoted enjoys some special "pull," the modern

[1] *About the Kinsey Report: Observations by Eleven Experts*, pp. 147, 148. (A Signet Special, published by the American Library of World Literature, New York.)

assumption is not that this unfortunate attitude is exclusively an on-the-job attitude. Instead, the assumption is that he would exhibit a similar attitude in any situation in which he was involved. The assumption, further, is that his attitude derives, not from inherent badness, nor from factual ignorance, but from some deep-lying emotional problem or set of problems that clutters up his life and prevents his full maturing—even though he may not consciously know that the problem is there.

III

Each of these three theories tends to carry itself out in its own characteristic way. Where the goodness-badness theory prevails, the methods of preachment, exhortation, rewards and punishments are used—often with more emphasis on punishments than on rewards. Where the knowledge-ignorance theory prevails, the methods are those of instruction, examination, and grading—of getting facts into minds and helping them to stay there. Where the maturity-immaturity theory begins to take hold, new methods emerge. These aim to help individuals to see their own lives whole; to recognize problem-points in those lives and to do something objective about them—in general, to move toward life with creative confidence, rather than away from it with fear and hostility.

The maturity-immaturity theory, because it calls for new methods, calls for a new kind of training for all those in a position to influence other lives. The task of our generation is not merely that of applying the maturity-immaturity concept, so that more people will have more awareness of what it means;

it is also that of maturing those who are to help others to mature. As parents, teachers, ministers, doctors, judges, lawyers, truant officers, prison wardens, foremen, supervisors, and all their fellows in power, have, in the past, variously—and too often detrimentally—applied the goodness-badness and the knowledge-ignorance theory of human behavior, so, now, they must be brought to the point of personal development where they can apply the more enlightened maturity-immaturity theory. If they are not brought to that point, the insights contributed by psychologists and psychiatrists can do little to give the needed new direction to our world. If, however, they can themselves become mature men and women, there is better hope for those who are within the range of their influential power.

It will mean much to our confused and hostility-ridden world if and when the conviction begins to dawn that the people we call "bad" are people we should call immature. This conviction would bring us to the realization of what needs to be done if our world is to be rescued from its many defeats. The chief job of our culture is, then, to help all people to grow up.

When he hung upon the cross, Christ is reported to have said one of the maturest things ever said by a suffering human being. While his torturers were making his last hours more terrible than they needed to have been by adding cruelty to cruelty, he prayed: "Father forgive them, for they know not what they do." He saw them not as "bad," but rather as too ungrown-up even to know that their cruelty was cruelty.

It is this insight—that the evil men do is the evil of their immaturity—that may yet save the world.

FOUR

MATURE INSIGHTS LOST ON IMMATURE MINDS

AS WE become familiar with the maturity concept, we find ourselves confronted by an old perplexity. The sound life as now described by psychologists and psychiatrists bears a strong resemblance to the sound life as long described by the greatest of our human seers and statesmen. The vocabulary is new. The clinical materials are new. The explanations of human misbehavior are, in many respects, new. Yet the type of relationship to life that is recommended by these modern scientists is surprisingly familiar: it has been recommended before. Time and again, throughout the centuries of human experience, it has been recommended by individuals who have seen more than those around them of how cause and effect work in the mental, emotional, and social affairs of men. Why, then, with these saving insights long since declared, do we continue to create misery for ourselves and others? All the necessary truths have been spoken. Many of them, in fact, are part of our daily speech; are said with reverence in our moments of worship; are, on great occasions, delivered as axioms of wisdom. Why have they been so relatively powerless to shape our daily behavior? Why have they not saved us?

One of our American poets, Edwin Arlington Robinson, has written:

> . . . we know the truth has been
> Told over to the world a thousand times;—
> But we have had no ears to listen yet
> For more than fragments of it; we have heard
> A murmur now and then, an echo here
> And there . . .[1]

This is what puzzles many of us: since we have long known the most inspired truths about human behavior and human relationships, why have we failed to put those truths into action?

Looked for in the light of our emergent psychological knowledge, the answer to our question stands clear: a mature truth told to immature minds ceases, in those minds, to be that same mature truth. Immature minds take from it only what immature minds can assimilate. In the end, even though they may give it lip-service and may raise institutions in its name, they turn the mature truth into an applied immaturity.

[1] From "Captain Craig," in *Collected Poems*, p. 116. Copyright, 1902, by Edwin Arlington Robinson. Used by permission of The Macmillan Company, publishers.

This fate of psychological depreciation has been the fate of all our greatest human truths. Uttered by mature minds, and for the purpose of maturing minds, they have been received, for the most part, by less mature minds—and have thus been only partially comprehended. Being only partially comprehended, they have found expression in ways that have perpetuated as much misunderstanding as understanding, as much error as truth.

Every great insight, we have heard it said, loses much of its greatness when it is institutionalized. One reason for this—perhaps the chief reason—is that the original insight becomes channeled to the human race through less mature people than those who first uttered it. The followers are less than the masters. The idea of human brotherhood, for example, which Jesus of Nazareth expressed with a superb passion, has become channeled through a multitude of followers so much less mature than he was that they have not actually known what he was talking about even when they have repeated his words. Thus an insight that might have saved the world has become largely a verbalism.

Brooks Adams coined the phrase, "the degradation of the democratic dogma." We might, in similar fashion, describe what has happened to great insights throughout history as the degradation of truth by minds too immature to understand it and put it into mature practice.

It is no new discovery that children only partially grasp most of what their parents try to tell them. Not at the first hearing nor at the tenth hearing do they fully understand what is said to them about the reasons for a certain rule of behavior, about the meaning of fairness and honesty and kindness, about the way in which human beings are linked together in destiny. Their ears may take in the words, and their tongues may learn to repeat them; but only as they themselves mature can they know with their whole make-up what the words really signify.

The limitations of the child-mind in the child-body are an old story. But only as we have come to know something about the problems of psychological growth have we been in a position to realize that similar limits are set to the reception of truth where childish outlooks and emotions are housed in an adult body. If there never yet have been "enough mature people in the right places," one of the places where there have never been enough of them has been *on the receiving end* of great truths. Because there have never been enough mature people to hear truth where it has been spoken, even the greatest of our truths have been in large measure impotent. Our insight into arrested development invites us, therefore, to a new appraisal of such significant insights as have come into human history. For now we have a way of doing justice to the greatness of what has been great, while, at the same time, we understand the failure of such greatness to effect our redemption from littleness.

II

A number of saving insights have been brought into the world without any of them saving the world.

The first of them was the novel idea of *One God*. The psychological drama of this idea has been well suggested by

Solomon Goldman, in his monumental study of the Old Testament:

> [The Bible] had its beginnings in the tales of a bold skeptic of whom it was recounted that, having rejected the beliefs universally adhered to in his day, he set out to transform the face of the earth. How he came by his skepticism or new faith is a question easier asked than answered . . . Of this much we are certain: once, in the ancient world, there lived a Jew, or one whom the Jews came to regard and claim as their own, who, repelled by idolatrous creeds and pagan practices, groped his way to a glimpse of the One God, perfect in all perfection.[2]

Here was a first essential human insight. As long as the belief in many gods prevailed—which was tantamount to a belief in many conflicting sources of truth—man could never free his mind from confusion. He could find no basis for consistent thought, no criterion for ethical evaluation, no ground for unity of judgment. Confronted by a multitude of gods, each claiming supremacy, and each clashing with others, man would continue to live in a world of mental, moral, and spiritual chaos.

That bold skeptic, whoever he was, brought a liberating insight: Truth is one because the Source of truth is one.

Now watch what happened to this great insight—again, as reported by Dr. Goldman:

> The people responded readily and agreed to do and obey. It resolved never again to be like unto the nations—but could

[2] Solomon Goldman, *The Book of Books,* p. ix. New York, Harper and Brothers, 1948.

not abandon their ways. It accepted the Eternal as God—but upon every hill and under every green tree it erected altars to wood and stone. It urged that man was God's image—but it would not abandon slavery . . . It longed for justice . . . but, fond of bribes, it neither judged the orphan nor did it plead the cause of the widow. It looked forward to peace but periodically became enmeshed in the web of imperialistic ambitions of Egypt, Assyria, or Babylon as the case might be. In a word, it dreamed of the ideal society and even legislated for it, but never got down to build it.

This story of a people's noble belief and ignoble backslidings; of its inspiring faith and its failure to live up to that faith; of its spiritual triumph and unspiritual self-defeats is the story of immature men incapable of grasping the fullness of the truth that had been offered to them. It is the story that has been acted out in thousandfold ways through the ages and far beyond the limits of that small tribe.

Nothing is more obvious than the almost universal degradation of the idea of the One God. In many cases, the Eternal One—the source of all truth—has been made into a jealous God, competing with other gods for man's favor; a whimful creature made in man's image; an angry old man, irritable in all-power, rather than serene in all-wisdom. In other cases, the One God has been made, not into an example of what man should reasonably *grow toward,* as he fulfills his powers, but into a mystery beyond man's comprehension—a mystery to paralyze man's mind. In yet other cases, the One God has been made into a tribal or national possession—a rallying point for nations in their wars with other nations.

Almost never in the thousands of years since this insight first came into the world has its original splendor been comprehended: the splendor of a reality without self-contradiction, one that can be understood and that responds to understanding; the splendor of a world not whimful, not broken up into clashing oppositions, but one that waits to reveal itself whole to the searching mind.

What is of particular moment to us, here, is not simply that man has failed fully to understand and act out the concept of One God, but that *he has failed in ways characteristic of immaturity*. His shortcomings in relation to this great insight do not so much mark him as a creature of evil, or of factual ignorance, as they suggest his being a creature who has habitually grown into adult stature and status without becoming mentally, emotionally, and socially mature.

In a home where children are getting their orientation toward life there may be one *father* in two entirely different senses of that term. There may be *one father* in the sense that there is a self-consistent directive influence—a person who himself does what he expects others to do; a person whose responses can be relied upon from day to day; a person who is *the same person* in relation to all the different children, not strict with one and indulgent of another. Or there may be *one father* in the sense that there is one person within the family group whose authority can never be questioned; whose whim is law; whose fluctuating moods create a kind of domestic weather to which all other individuals must adjust; who gives and withholds favors as he happens to feel like giving or withholding them; who plays favorites if he wants to do so, because he is above the law; and for whom the arch crime that a child could commit would be to grow into the kind of independence that would make him show a mind of his own and rebel against his father's authority.

Where there is *one father* in this latter sense, there is, we have come to know, almost a guarantee that the children will grow up without becoming fully mature. Even in their adulthood, they will have no genius for equality. Whether they become irrationally rebellious or irrationally submissive, the strongest force in their lives will be, not their own productive urge to life, but their relationship to authority. Most of them, in all likelihood, will become people who look up to those in power and, within their own limited areas of authority, try to imitate such power. They will be emotionally unstable, emotionally dependent, and, like children, inclined to alternate between a fear-ridden reverence in the presence of their chosen authority and a belligerent, false courage in the presence of other grown-up children: "My father can lick your father with one hand tied behind his back!"

Presented with the sublime, self-consistent idea of One God, men whose own experience had kept them largely immature in their relationship to authority proceeded to convert that One God into a whimful, tribal tyrant—a tyrant before whom they must tremble; whose word they must obey whether or not it comported with rationality; but whom, by way of compensation, they could call *their own,* thereby claiming part of his strength as theirs.

That the *One God* is today still many gods—many different gods in many different possessive minds—is a measure of our continued immaturity. That the One God, instead of being a source of peace, has been a source of fratricidal war, indicates how far short we have fallen of being fully developed in our human powers.

III

For a second insight we are indebted to this same people: *man is a creature of moral law.*

The picture of Moses descending from Mt. Sinai bearing the tablets of the law is a symbol of the revelation to man of his own uniquely human nature. Animals know no moral law. For countless ages, man himself knew no moral law. In those animal-like ages, his self-restraints were those of custom, not of understanding in the area of social cause and effect. His relations with his fellows were instinctual, not moral.

Because, in the days of the legendary Moses, men were still mostly immature, morality was first expressed as commands: *Thou shalt not.* But the moral insight of this legendary figure was so genuine that the commands he issued as from God came not as the whimful and arbitrary dictates of a tyrant, but rather as the voice of moral reason itself. The things that were commanded were right and necessary if men were to live together in peace and justice. To lie, steal, covet, commit adultery, dishonor the older members of the group, worship idols, deny a day of rest—these things, practiced widely and with impunity, would make impossible the sort of social structure within which men could live with confidence. The "Thou shalt nots," in brief, were the revelation of what man, in his moral reason, would himself refuse to do if he truly knew himself.

The Decalogue remains for us the first great insight of our culture into man's moral nature. There had been other "codes" before this one, but they had lacked the consistency of moral insight conveyed in the Decalogue. One and all, they had been class codes, making arbitrary discriminations between human beings; assigning more rights to some than to others. Thus, they were not yet moral because they failed of moral universality. They belonged to cultures that had not yet emerged from the stage of many gods and many different truths: one truth for the highborn, another for the lowborn. The Decalogue was the first statement of the oneness of all who are human: oneness in rights and oneness in obligations.

But here again the story repeats itself: the story of a great truth brought down to the level of immaturity.

What immature minds have done to the Decalogue has been, first of all, to turn it from a series of universal principles into a series of taboos. This has notoriously happened in the case of Sabbath observance. The deep reason for a time of rest is obvious. The fact that this time of rest must be so regularly established that it cannot be denied to any one— even the humblest worker—is likewise obvious. But time and again, the admonition to observe the Sabbath has been turned into the prohibition of even the most necessary and life-preserving work. By the time of Christ, for example, taboo had so far concealed the original purpose of the law that the priests found it necessary to reprimand him for curing a man's illness on the Sabbath day. Again, the observance of the Sabbath has divided people into those who tenaciously hold that God had appointed one certain day of the week and those who as tenaciously hold that he had appointed another.

Again, "Thou shalt not bear false witness" has been turned, among other things, into a taboo-ceremony in courts of law. The implication is that God may strike you dead if you bear false witness *with your hand on the Bible*—the further implication being that if you merely lie, without swearing on the Bible that you are telling the truth, you will be in no such danger.

What immature minds have done to the Decalogue has been, in the second place, to give it so narrow and literal an interpretation that it has been largely robbed of its power to encourage man toward moral maturity. "Thou shalt not steal" has been chiefly interpreted to mean that you must not overtly take what obviously belongs to somebody else. Most of the subtler forms of stealing, however—through the adulteration of goods, for example; through financial manipulations of the market; through imperialism—have been given other names than stealing and have been largely ignored.

The same has been true in the case of the admonitions against lying, killing, committing adultery, coveting. Arthur Hugh Clough, in his new *Decalogue*, has pointedly suggested how the narrow, literal interpretation of these moral commands has failed to reach the full-scale immoralities that are part of the going concern we call civilization:

> Thou shalt not covet, but tradition
> Approves all forms of competition;

Thou shalt not kill, but needst not strive
Officiously to keep alive.[3]

We do not know how deeply the man known as Moses
may have penetrated to the core of these moral laws; but we
do know that through subsequent history immature minds
have taken from them little more than their surface meanings.
It still remains for the world to learn what the Ten Command-
ments really report about the essentials of human nature.
Until the time of our greater maturing, the Decalogue will
remain an ambiguous presence in our midst: on the one hand,
a liberating revelation of the means by which men may live
together with mutual confidence; on the other a set of taboos
that have the power to control behaviors only within the most
narrow and literal definitions, and that divide men along the
lines of fanatical interpretations rather than unite them in a
common insight.

IV

Amos, the peasant-prophet, spoke ringing words:

Hear this word, ye kine of Bashan, that are in the mountain of
Samaria, which oppress the poor, which crush the needy, which
say to their masters, Bring, and let us drink.

The Lord God hath sworn by his holiness, that lo, the days shall
come upon you, that he will take you away with hooks, and your
posterity with fishhooks.

[3] Arthur Hugh Clough, "The Latest Decalogue," from *Poems*. New York,
The Macmillan Company.

Here, in the words of an angry man, we read another of the world's great insights: that there must be an end to special privilege and to the exploitation of the weak by the strong; that social justice must come; that the demand for such justice is not an arbitrary human demand, but so inherent in the structure of man's relationship to man that to flout it is to invite disaster.

In most of the ancient world—Egypt, Assyria, Babylonia, and the oriental despotisms—the plea for social justice had not only not yet been heard, but if it had been spoken, it would have been met with instant punishment. The thought that the ordinary human being had a right to humane treatment and a right to just treatment was far removed from these empires of caprice and arbitrary power. It remained for a few rare persons, socially mature beyond their time and beyond their fellows, to pour out their indignation in behalf of the dispossessed and the helpless. It remained for an Amos, a Micah, an Isaiah to speak for civilization in a world of moral barbarism.

"Learn to do well; seek judgment, relieve the oppressed, judge the fatherless, plead for the widow," cried Isaiah. And Micah summed up the whole duty of man when he said, "He hath shewed thee, O man, what is good . . . what doth the Lord require of thee, but to do justly, and to love mercy, and to walk humbly with thy God?"

Here, then, was another great insight: man, by virtue of his status as a human being in the universe, is under obligation to consider his fellow man and treat him well—the fellow man who is poor no less than the one who is rich; the helpless no less than the powerful.

This insight required more of the individual than did the "Thou shalt nots" of the Decalogue. It required a live imagination about other people: the sort of empathic imagination that is still only a potential in the child and that can come to its fullness only as the child matures. The power to feel another's hurt and to want to heal that hurt, to sense another's need and to want to satisfy that need—this is the root of social justice. Without it, not even the strictest law can cause justice or mercy to triumph as a social force over the will to self-advantage.

Later, the full implication of this thought was seen by another peasant-prophet, Jesus of Nazareth, when in a flash of inspiration, he laid down the rule basic to all moral life: "Do unto others as ye would that others do unto you." Jesus was here asking of man something far removed from the child's ego-absorption. He was asking the mature power to see others with the same honest concern with which one sees oneself.

And now again came the story of defeat. These prophets did not wholly succeed even with their own people—much less with the whole world. Their years of prophesying were spent in passionate and perilous denunciation of oppressors who would not listen. "Let judgment run down as the waters," cried Amos, "and righteousness as a mighty stream." But judgment did not run down as the waters nor righteousness as a mighty stream. The big oppressors and the little oppressors continued largely as before.

"Then I said, Lord, how long? And he answered, Until the cities be wasted without inhabitant, and the houses without men, and the land be utterly desolate."

Social justice still goes largely unfulfilled. Today, however, we can perhaps speak a new word about the reason for its long unfulfillment. The simple fact is that social justice requires of man a fuller growth out of the egocentricity of childhood than he has yet achieved. Immature life is life in which imagination has not yet stretched to take in the wants and needs of other people. It is therefore moved chiefly by the vivid urgency of its own self-concern: self-concern in the most immediate and limited sense of the word, not in the great sense of self-fulfillment. While our proper destiny as individuals is to grow beyond the egocentricity of childhood into the inclusive sociocentricity of the mature, most of us—and most of our forebears throughout history—have largely failed thus to grow up.

Today, we might well ask with the prophet Amos, "Lord, how long?" And we might well believe that the only alternative answer to the grim words, "Until the cities be wasted without inhabitant," is the psychological insight, "Until man grows into emotional and social maturity."

V

In some respects, the most audacious of all the great insights that have come into the world was the apparently absurd conviction of Jesus of Nazareth that men must love one another. "A new commandment I give unto you that ye love one another." We can easily imagine the bewilderment—

even the ribald laughter—of his hearers. A world that was still very far from reaching the level of universal justice could scarcely rise to the level of universal love.

In reality, this "new commandment" was not an absurd and arbitrary rule laid upon man from the outside. It was, rather, the most profound insight into man's nature that had yet been achieved. Today every psychiatrist would affirm its truth. Man is sound in psychological health to the degree that he relates himself affirmatively to his fellow men. To hate and to fear is to be psychologically ill.

This is an illness, however, that still widely afflicts us. It is, in fact, the consuming illness of our time. "The only real threat to man," writes G. B. Chisholm, ". . . is man himself . . . the difficulty man has with himself is that he cannot use his highly developed intellect effectively because of his neurotic fears, his prejudices, his fanaticisms, his unreasoning hates, and equally unreasoning devotions; in fact, his failure to reach emotional maturity, or mental health." [4]

With the audacity of a logic larger and deeper than they were prepared to understand, the Nazarene spoke to his fellow men: "Love your enemies, do good to them that hate you. Bless them that curse you, and pray for them that despitefully use you. And to him that smiteth thee on one cheek offer also the other; and him that taketh away thy cloke forbid not to take the coat also." This must have sounded like utter nonsense. It still sounds like nonsense to those who have not entered the new dimension of life conceived by the speaker: the dimension in which *man affirms his fellow man*.

This is what love means, whether spoken by Jesus or by the

[4] *Survey Graphic*, October 1947.

most modern of psychiatrists. The love of a person implies, not the possession of that person, but the affirmation of that person. It means granting him, gladly, the full right to his unique humanhood. One does not truly love a person and yet seek to enslave him—by law or by bonds of dependence and possessiveness.[5]

Whenever we experience a genuine love, we are moved by this transforming experience toward a capacity for good will. Or we might put the matter inversely: if what we call love in relation to one person or to a few people creates in us nc added capacity for good will toward many, then we may doubt that we have actually experienced love. In all likelihood, what we have experienced is some form of immature ego-aggrandizement or some equally immature will to make security for ourselves in a dangerous world by clinging to the role of the dependent.

Most people—and this applies as much to those who call themselves Christians as to others—have grown to adulthood without developing a generous, spontaneous capacity to love: to affirm others. Instead, they have grown to adulthood carrying with them fears and hostilities born of childhood failures and intensified by a continued effort to effect a childish, not a responsible and mature, relationship to life. By and large, they have been unable to apply the insight of Jesus of Nazareth because what they have called love, even in their most intimate associations, has not been love.

Today, continues Chisholm the psychiatrist, with sharp urgency:

[5] The psychiatrist, Eric Fromm, has developed this idea with notable effectiveness in his book, *Man for Himself.*

In order that the human race may survive on this planet, it is necessary that there should be enough people in enough places in the world who do not have to fight each other, who are not the kinds of people who will fight each other, and who are the kinds of people who will take effective measures whenever it is necessary to prevent other people's fighting.

In short, smiting each other on the cheek, and smiting back, actually does not work—however highly an immature world may rate it, as "common sense." It is common nonsense. Therefore, "a new commandment I give unto you"—to develop enough emotional maturity to take the initiative in breaking the vicious circle of smiting and being smitten. This is the commandment—laid upon man by his own social nature—that has, more than any other, been given lip-service and then disobeyed in action. It has been disobeyed because those who have given it lip-service have too often been too immature to act it out or even to understand its deeper implications. They have thought that it required them to deny their own nature, or, by some divine grace, to transcend that nature; they have not realized that what it asked was a mature fulfillment of that nature.

VI

To the Greeks we owe another insight: that man is a rational animal and that his fulfillment calls for the exercise of his reason. Reasoning is the principle that brings order: that turns confusion into clarity, formlessness into form. It selects, relates, organizes; out of chaos it creates a universe.

Reason, however, the Greek thinkers saw, is a *capacity* in man, not necessarily an achievement. In most men it lies largely dormant while something else, which is far from reason, takes over. Socrates spent a lifetime revealing to his fellow Athenians that what they thought was the exercise of reason was actually the exercise of unreason. Therefore— as though, perversely, to prove themselves as unreasonable as he said they were—they put him to death.

The tale of this insight follows the pattern of the others. What the Greek thinkers saw was true: man is at his best when he exercises the power of reason. To the extent that he is unreasonable—a creature of impulse, of prejudice, of rationalizations—he passes judgments and performs actions that do not comport with the realities of his environment. Therefore, in a multitude of ways, he does what he ought not to have done and leaves undone what he ought to have done— thereby compounding friction rather than harmony, error rather than truth. The person who lives by unreason, in brief, fails to utilize the one power by which man is enabled to effect a partial escape from sheer subjectivity and to enter into the same objective world that other people inhabit; the one power by which he is enabled to escape from the immediate and to enter into the longer time-span which embraces past, present, and future in an over-all design of cause and effect; the one power by which he is enabled to shake off the merely customary in favor of the ideal. The insight was true— but there were few in Greece, or anywhere else, who were mature enough to prefer rationality to irrationality.

In Greece, as elsewhere, most minds had blundered so far

into the territory of unreason that they not only could not find their way out, but could not even glimpse enough of reason to feel dissatisfied with the contrast it presented. The infantilisms revealed all through Greek political history, culminating in the fratricidal Peloponnesian wars that brought the doom of their civilization—these show only too clearly that the Greeks were not, as a people, ready to understand the few great thinkers who lived among them, who spoke the words which, properly understood, might have saved them, and who still speak clearly, down through the ages, to the minds of all rational men.

So again, as in other cases, mature insight suffered the fate visited upon it by variously immature minds. The power to see what-follows-from-what is, as we have already noted, a power than an infant does not possess and that a child possesses only in very limited degree. It is, in brief, a mature power. It depends upon the mental accumulation of data that it takes time and experience for a human being to collect. It depends, also, upon a mental orderliness and discipline that are the fruits of more sustained effort and observation than any child has yet put forth.

The power of reason is the power to see logical implications: of similarity and difference, of cause and effect, of relationships in time and space, of quantity and quality, of the subjective and the objective, of importance and unimportance. The human mind has, as one of its most unique potentials, the capacity to see such logical implications. If it develops healthily from infancy through childhood, and on into adulthood, this inborn capacity becomes a more and more adequately developed tool for use. But, as we have observed, this growth toward mental maturity is not automatic. It may be checked by emotional road-blocks. The individual, for example, will not develop his powers of reason in all their fullness if, by so doing, he would be forced to relinquish a position of emotional dependence that has become indispensable to him. Neither will he develop such powers if, by so doing, he would be forced to see his own brand of prestige and success as a petty thing, his own ambition as a ruthless will to dominate others at whatever cost to their welfare. In such instances, the individual does not reason; he rationalizes —thereby pretending to himself that he obeys the dictates of his mind when, in actuality, he obeys the dictates of his unconscious and of the unresolved emotional problems lodged in that unconscious. Anyone who threatens to expose his self-deception—to reveal him as he is, in all his irrationality—becomes, to his mind, an archenemy: a Socrates whose disturbing voice must be silenced. As most people come to their adulthood bringing with them various unconscious reasons for not wanting to be mature, most people have had only a reluctant ear for the voice of reason; and the gift of insight offered to man by the greatest of the Greeks, and by similar minds throughout the centuries, has been more often rejected than received.

VII

Another insight into man's nature was variously expressed during the Renaissance. In those years, men were beginning to be restive under old authority. They had been tied long enough to theological dogmas. They had been pigeonholed long enough in the status-cubicles provided for them by feudalism. A liberating conviction was growing among men that man must discover his own destiny—not in a distant heaven, but on earth—and that his destiny must express what he is as an individual, not what he is as a member of a certain social or economic class.

The Renaissance was an affirmation of individuality. It bade the human find within himself the creative sources of his own fulfillment. In this respect, the Renaissance was a necessary and salutary revolt against medieval authoritarianism. It was, we might say, man the adolescent emerging out of the long dependence of infancy and childhood. But it was not yet man the mature adult.

The insight that invited the human being to become acquainted with his individual earthly self and to make independent creative use of the powers he discovered within himself was a mature insight. But, received largely by adolescent minds, it was given at most an adolescent interpretation. When we say that most of the minds that welcomed it were adolescent rather than mature, we mean that they were ready to assert their independence but that they were, as yet, inexperienced in the uses, the triumphs, and the hazards of independence. Having made good, as it were, their rebellion against parental authority, they found themselves free—and unsure. With outside barriers to their maturing largely removed, they were still confronted by barriers within themselves: habits and attitudes which they had carried over from the time when they were living within a dogma-system and a status-system and which left them ill-equipped to fill with mature content their brave new assertion of individuality.

This accounts, on the one hand, for most of the extravagances, false starts, instabilities, and caprices of Renaissance creativity—for to be creative without a sure, directive purpose is to be undisciplined from the inside. It is, all too often, to become fixated at an adolescent level of self-awareness.

The fact that the demand for *freedom from* did not carry with it a clear sense of *freedom for* accounts, also, for the promptness and the terrible dogmatism with which many of the minds released from medievalism hurried to take refuge in a new absolute. The Reformation, as the religious phase of the Renaissance, invited man to become just independent enough to take the step from one orthodoxy into another. It emphatically did not invite him to become genuinely mature in his spiritual independence. Here again we note the adolescent character of the period. The adolescent who breaks away from parental authority is by no means ready to make his own choices and decisions. He is, on the contrary, one of the most rigid conformists that we know anything about. He takes the one independent step that carries him out of the family value-system only to adopt the rigidly intolerant value-system of his own age group. Later, if he is to become mature, he must take the confident additional steps that lead to independence of judgment.

VIII

The most recent of the great insights that have invited man to maturity came with the development of science. The scientific method is not commonly regarded as an insight into human nature; but this, in its essence, is what it is. It is a systematized expression of the fact that man is a species capable of transcending his own limitations of sense and of subjectivity.

The scientific insight, like the other great insights we have examined, came into a world unprepared for it. The fate suffered by Roger Bacon is a vivid revelation of the state of mind that existed when science was making its first hesitant entrance. To remind us of that fate, I quote here from Andrew D. White, in his *History of the Warfare of Science and Theology:*

> The first great thinker . . . who persevered in a truly scientific path was Roger Bacon . . . He wrought with power in many sciences, and his knowledge was sound and exact . . . In his writings are found formulae for extracting phosphorus, manganese, and bismuth. It is even claimed, with much appearance of justice, that he investigated the power of steam, and he seems to have very nearly reached some of the principal doctrines of modern chemistry. But it should be borne in mind that his *method* of investigation was even greater than its *results*. In an age when theological subtilizing was alone thought to give the title of scholar, he insisted on *real* reasoning and the aid of natural science by mathematics; in an age when experimenting was sure to cost a man his reputation, and was likely to cost him his life, he insisted on experimenting, and braved all its risks. Few greater men have lived.
>
> On this man came the brunt of the battle. The most conscientious men of his time thought it their duty to fight him, and they

fought him steadily and bitterly . . . He was attacked and condemned mainly because he did not believe that philosophy had become complete, and that nothing more was to be learned . . .

But this was not the worst; another theological idea was arrayed against him—the idea of Satanic intervention in science . . .

The most powerful protectors availed him little. His friend, Guy of Foulques, having in 1265 been made Pope under the name of Clement IV, shielded him for a time; but the fury of the enemy was too strong, and when he made ready to perform a few experiments before a small audience, we are told that all Oxford was in an uproar. It was believed that Satan was about to be let loose. Everywhere priests, monks, fellows, and students rushed about, their garments streaming in the wind, and everywhere rose the cry, "Down with the magician!" and this cry, "Down with the magician!" resounded from cell to cell and from hall to hall.[6]

This story does more than report an event. It pictures the immaturity of most minds at the time when science was making its entry and developing its method. It shows those minds to have been terrified by the unfamiliar. It shows them also to have been ready to strike out in irrational fear-bred rage at that which seemed a threat to their own security and prestige. It shows them, most of all, to have been trapped within a set of beliefs and superstitions that forbade their becoming mature: that made it heresy for them to use their minds except within limits approved by the "parental authority" of the church.

[6] Andrew D. White, *History of the Warfare of Science and Theology*, vol. 1, p. 385. Copyright by Appleton-Century-Crofts, Inc., New York.

Yet science eventually made its way into the world. Then the second thing happened to prevent its insight from working its full effects: the *results* of science were taken over by the many; but the *method* of science was left to the few, although it was in the application of the *method*, not in the mere using of the *results*, that there lay the richest promise of man's maturing. We know the story now. The veriest fool can use the most brilliant results of scientific experiment. The criminal can use them in his moral immaturity and perversity. To pull the lever, to push the button, to turn the dial, to shift the gears—these acts require no mature knowledge, no sense of responsibility, no empathy, no philosophic sense of the *whole*. They can be performed in the service of childish egocentricity and ego-aggrandizement no less than in the service of mature sociocentricity.

Thus, while the inventions of science magnify the power of the immature no less than the power of the mature—and magnify it to a point where a few childish minds can destroy the world—the insight of science remains unrealized. *Man is a creature capable of so transcending his own limitations of sense and of subjectivity as to gain ever more knowledge about his world and about himself in that world.* This is the insight that invites man to maturity. Also, it is an insight still uncomprehended, still largely ignored.

IX

In the second half of the eighteenth century two dramatic insights burst upon the horizon. They were expressed in two notable phrases: "created equal" and "consent of the governed." The first repudiated the ancient assumption that man is born into the world wearing a badge of class. The second affirmed the right of all men to have a voice in determining the political structure under which they are to live.

Not surprisingly the two notions were laughed to scorn by those conditioned to the acceptance of class superiority and government by force. Yet they prevailed with a sufficient strength to bring into existence a new kind of government and a new order of legal rights: democratic government and civil rights.

There is every indication that both insights are true. Class-tags are man-made conventions. The psychological differences that exist among men recommend their being given opportunities suited to their individual needs; those differences do not recommend the stratification of the human race along the ancient lines of privilege, power, and nationality. They do not indicate that some are born to be slaves, while others are born to be free; that some are born to be governed, while others are born to govern.

The announcement of the democratic insight did not, however, guarantee its being understood and acted upon with mature responsibility and imagination. Even the creation of a society to embody the insight and to give it legal standing did not so guarantee. Nothing is more clear than that the destiny of the democratic insight depends upon the mental, emotional, and social maturity of the people who make up the democracy. Thus far, every democracy on earth has been only a partial success because it has had only a partially mature citizenship through which to be realized. The happiest thing, in fact, that can be said about democracy, from a psychological angle, is that it is one of the few systems that has ever been willing to risk a long period of confusion and mixed purposes for the sake of giving man a chance to grow up in mind and in responsibility as well as in body. Because it has been willing to run this risk, it may yet produce enough mature people to insure its own continuity and further growth.

X

As we look back upon these major truths that have come into the world, we realize what maturity might have done with them. This, too, we realize: if we could only find a way of making ourselves mature, we could pick up these lost parts of ourselves and make them come alive. There is no other way; for immaturity has the inevitable power to make immature application of even the most mature insights. As long as so many of us continue to be immature in our linkages with life—arrested at the level of infancy, childhood, or adolescence—so long will the great insights be powerless to save the world.

Here is the clue-insight through which all the other insights may, in the end, be brought to their realization; the clue-insight without which all the others are lost: *the psychological growth of man must keep pace with his physical powers; every increase in power must be matched by an increase in understanding.*

Psychology and psychiatry, as we have noted, are offering us a new standard by which we may come to a new self-awareness and, thereby, a new maturity. We have, so far in this book, tried to gain a working familiarity with that standard. In the chapters that follow we shall try to measure, by our psychological yardstick, the practices and institutions that play upon our lives and that encourage us to full development of our powers or to an arrested development.

PART TWO

FORCES THAT SHAPE US

FIVE

A HERITAGE OF CONTRADICTIONS

THOSE WHO live within a culture breathe in its philosophic atmosphere as inevitably as they breathe in the environing air. If that atmosphere is clear and wholesome, it will be conducive to their philosophical—and therefore their psychological—growth. The philosophical atmosphere of our time is not clear and wholesome. It does not, accordingly, encourage a full maturing of the many millions who breathe it in—and take it for granted.

A philosophic atmosphere may be unwholesome in two respects. It may contain such contradictory elements that those who live within it almost inevitably come to a state of inner contradiction. It may, again, be unwholesome because it actually sets a premium on the prolongation of immaturity. The philosophic atmosphere of our time is unwholesome in both respects.

If our times are out of joint, it is because they are *philo-*

sophically out of joint. If we are to set them right, we shall have to set them philosophically right. We shall, in brief, have to create for ourselves a philosophic outlook for ourselves that is, first of all, consistent—free of inner contradictions; and, second, an encouragement to the mature development of our human powers.

II

Three major strains in our cultural philosophy compete for dominance. In certain times and places, they engage in open warfare. In others, they exist side by side in a state of uneasy truce. In yet others, they engage in a hearty and superficial pretense that, in spite of minor differences, they all belong to one big happy family. Their warfare, their uneasy truces, and their sophistic agreements are reflected, in some measure, in the practices of our every institution—social, political, economic, educational, religious—and in the behaviors of every member of our culture.

The first strain is that of *authoritarianism*, both religious and political. Strict orthodoxy—whether Catholic, Protestant, or of some other sort—encourages a certain type of character structure. The "believer" is rated as sincere and wholehearted to the extent that he takes things on faith and exempts certain areas of experience from critical examination. To the extent that he is thus "sound," he leaves to some vested authority—priest, minister, or other—the major responsibility of defining his spiritual responsibility. Thus, in a double sense, he is invited to remain immature: mentally, in that he foregoes his human right to ask, as an individual, certain questions that have tantalized the mind of man ever since he became man; and emotionally, in that he accepts a basic spiritual dependence as his lifelong estate. The rewards offered him for being thus a "believer" also tend to perpetuate his psychological childhood: on the one hand, he is permitted, during his term on earth, to feel himself a member of the "elect," different from the unregenerate crowd of people variously lost in error; and on the other hand, he is permitted to anticipate a sort of cosmic accolade that will be his private own through a perpetual and unsharing bliss.

Political authoritarianism has taken the form of an increasing dominance of the state in the life of the individual. Nationalism in its beginnings was a liberating force; but it was not long before the development of nations into super-powers competing with one another for territory and prestige turned them into vast military and economic mechanisms controlling the life of their citizens. The "freedom" of the citizen became a freedom to do what his nation permitted him to do. What the nation demanded of its members was the kind of instant and unquestioning loyalty that could be depended upon in its struggles with other nations.

"Patriotism" has, for the most part, taken forms that have encouraged uncritical adherence to the policies of one's own nation—"my country right or wrong"—and a blunting of the imagination as to the needs, rights, and attitudes of the people of other nations. The effect of the nationalistic patriotisms has been to discourage linkages of understanding, sympathy, and co-operation with other nations—and with the people of those nations—and to encourage the kind of exclusiveness that fosters suspicion and hostility.

Political authoritarianism is now in such full swing that "government" has, even in the democratic nations, become the supreme arbiter of the life of the individual. In the major matters of life and death, occupation, and reputation, the state rules; and the individual is helpless to resist that rule.

Thus the strain of authoritarianism in our culture—whether religious or political or both—has been powerful to hold the average individual in a condition of immature dependence. In the chief matters of his concern he has had to learn how to forego independence of judgment and creative initiative and be willing to accept life as fashioned for him by powers that claim his grateful adherence but deny him the right to think freely for himself.

The second major strain in our culture is that of intellectual, political, and social *liberalism*. This was primarily a gift of the eighteenth century, the period of the "enlightenment." It was the special genius of the enlightenment that it effected the marriage of two older strains both of which aimed at the dignifying and maturing of human nature: the strain of social religion, as this runs like a golden thread through the Old Testament and through the teachings of Jesus; and the strain of classic faith in the rationality of man.

Liberalism, like authoritarianism, encourages its own type of character structure. It invites man to try to understand the physical-spiritual workings of the universe and to work out, first, a relationship to that universe that comports with his creative human status and, second, a relationship to his fellow man that will express in practice his conviction of human dignity. It invites him to feel, moreover, not the sinfulness and worthlessness of man, but the high powers of sociality and rationality that exist in man and bid for release. Liberalism asked man to grow up to the full stature of a self-governing and self-fulfilling human being.

If there is one concourse of historic events for which we in America should be more deeply grateful than for any other, it is that the American colonies were ready for independence and for the shaping of their major institutions at a time when liberalism was stronger than at almost any other time before or after. Not that the liberal spirit and the sense of human dignity have always been triumphant in our culture, nor have they effected any unanimous transformation of all individuals and institutions; but, in peculiarly happy degree, those who have been on the side of man's maturing have had a kind of support in American tradition and institution that could not be wholly withdrawn even in the darkest periods of reaction.

The third strain in our culture is that of nineteenth-century *mechanism* and antirationalism. We tend, in our common thinking, to take it for granted that our culture has had a coherent, unbroken development that has carried it, with a few minor setbacks, toward the ideals declared in its original documents. This assumption of consistency and progress has largely blinded us to the fact that *the major philosophies of the nineteenth century not only did not support, but actually contradicted, that major philosophy under which our political institutions were framed.* The chief philosophies of the eighteenth century saw man as possessing a dignity that required him to claim and defend such rights as would give him and his fellows a chance to grow in mental grasp and social responsibility. The chief philosophies of the nineteenth century saw man, on the contrary, as largely the creation of mechanical and subrational forces; and the "rights" that they granted him were less those of rational growth than of self-aggrandizement. Even the optimism of the century was irrational. Whether based on a misinterpretation of Darwin's thesis of the survival of the fittest, or on the theory of "automatic progress," this optimism largely divorced the betterment of human society from the exercise of human rationality and social responsibility. Mechanism and antirationalism, like the other philosophic strains we have mentioned, encouraged a certain type of character structure. It was not a mature type. Whereas authoritarianism had invited man to remain a child in spiritual and political dependence, the philosophies of the nineteenth century invited him to remain a child in aggressive egocentricity.

We shall wish to examine in greater detail this contradictory century that preceded our own. Before we turn in this detailed examination, we must ask briefly why the obvious contradictions in our threefold philosophic heritage have not been widely detected.

It takes a *whole* person to feel keenly the absence of *wholeness,* and a mature person to feel keenly what is lost to life where maturity is never experienced. The simple fact is that comparatively few among us have been either whole or mature; for all of us have, in greater or lesser degree, been conditioned since birth by personalities and institutions that have themselves been prey to inner contradictions.

The situation would be less complex if certain of our institutions did a clear job of embodying any one of our three major philosophical strains, while other institutions, with equal clarity and conviction, embodied the others. Then we would see the differences being acted out before our eyes. Then we would almost inevitably measure and compare and choose. But nowhere in our society can we point to any institution that is philosophically simon-pure. No church gives unadulterated and undisguised expression to the philosophy of authoritarianism: through the mixed conditioning of its leaders and communicants, even the most orthodox has been somewhat influenced by both liberalism and the nineteenth-century brand of antirationalism. No economic institution, though it may plead its cause in the idiom of nineteenth-century individualism, is wholly exempt from the influence of authoritarian religion and eighteenth-century liberalism. What is true of the church and the economic order is true no less of the home, the school, and the political order. In each of these we see a warfare of philosophies, or a truce among philosophies, or a pretense of wholeness where wholeness does not exist. Unless we understand this deep confusion that marks our culture—and that therefore marks our minds—we cannot begin to understand either the clarifying hope that is introduced by the maturity concept or the difficulties that lie in the way of the full and fruitful acceptance of that concept.

III

A short analysis of something as complex as a century of human life—and, in particular, a century of change—is bound to be oversimple. Yet if we take even a brief look at the nineteenth century, with eyes that have borrowed insight from the psychologists and psychiatrists, we seem to discover that the philosophies that came to dominate that century—and in large measure, so far, our own twentieth century—did not encourage human maturing. The most mature social developments of the century, in fact, drew their ideational support from older philosophies: those of social religion and of political liberalism.

I remember my student days in Weimar, Germany, walking past a barred window of the house where the "mad philosopher," Nietzsche, lived. Even then he was a legend and a power for the future. German students carried his *Thus Spake Zarathustra* in their pockets. They quoted from his *Anti-Christ,* his *Will to Power,* and his *Beyond Good and Evil.* They spoke witheringly of mercy and pity; mocked the "slave morality" that the meek Jew of Nazareth had recommended; proclaimed the doctrine of the Superman—the individual who was "beyond good and evil." To be hard, heroic, fearless, disregardful of the "many too many" that cluttered up the earth—this was the new "good news" for which they thanked their prophet, Nietzsche.

The term "mad philosopher" was peculiarly apt as applied to Nietzsche. Edwin Arlington Robinson has observed that

The man who goes too far alone goes mad—
In one way or another.[1]

What Nietzsche exemplified in his own life, and recommended to other men, was precisely the act of going "too far alone." He was justified in his rejection of the handwashing subservience that marked too many of the people around him. He was justified, likewise, in his conviction that individual man must affirm himself, not abase himself, if he is to have dignity. But he seems to have missed the significant fact that man is a creature of mutual attachments and responsibilities: that he becomes himself, not in the role of superman—since, for better or worse, he was born *man*— but through the mutually affirmative linkages he establishes with other people. In a profound psychological sense, his philosophy was an invitation to madness—the madness of a greater isolation than human stuff can tolerate; and in a profound historical sense, it was typical of the philosophies that peculiarly marked the nineteenth century. In one thought-system after another, we find the taint of the same madness: the insistence that individual man or some special portion of humanity—race, nation, or economic class—can go it alone; can act out the role of superman. Such philosophic "madness" does not foster maturity.

In Nietzsche, it was the individual superman who was to go it alone, splendid in solitary pride. In the works of certain other German philosophers, this role was assigned to a super-

[1] From "Merlin," in *Collected Poems*, p. 254. Copyright, 1917, by The Macmillan Company and used by their permission.

people, a super-race, a super-nation. Thus Fichte, in his *Speeches to the German People,* attributed "everything original which is not deadened by arbitrary regulations" to the Germans, and declared everything else to be foreign. "To have a character," he wrote, "and to be German mean beyond doubt the same." He proved to his own complete satisfaction —and that of a host of followers—that the German language is the only "genuine language" and that the Germans alone are "truly a people." Even Hegel, *magister* of world dialectic, designated the Prussian state as the point of cosmic fulfillment.

Fichte and Hegel exerted a compelling influence upon the minds of both German thinkers and students from abroad who, in those days, flocked to the German universities to do advanced work in philosophy. What they had to say, moreover, about the superiority of the German people was repeated and developed—with a lesser show of logic and a greater show of fanaticism—by minor figures who were enough in tune with the spirit of the times to gain a far wider audience than they deserved.

Thus, Schleiermacher said that "only here in the Fatherland do you find in profusion everything that adorns mankind." [2] Houston Chamberlain, a German with an English name, made out of spurious anthropology a philosophy that subsequently carried as much weight as though the science on which it rested had been sound. He "proved" that the German race was the one pure and superior race and that it must, at all costs, be kept so. His doctrines of race and anti-Semitism

---

[2] *See* Paul Roubiczek, *The Misinterpretation of Man,* p. 68. New York, Charles Scribner's Sons, 1947.

did not fall on deaf ears. Instead, those who heard were, in multitude, ready to believe—or to half-believe. And those who heard were not only Germans but students from all the other countries of Europe and from America. Racism and intense nationalism—with their declaration that only some selected part of mankind is fit for leadership—not only took obvious command of many nineteenth-century minds but effected a subtle invasion of uncounted others.

In another country, and another area of thought, Adam Smith contributed likewise to the "madness" of a century in which too many men tried to go "too far alone"; for while Adam Smith died ten years before the end of the eighteenth century, it was in the nineteenth century that his economic philosophy took command of the minds and institutions of men. With or without him, a new way of economic life would have come; for powerful forces of science and technology had made a crumbling feudalism impotent either to control or to release the energies of men. What Adam Smith did was to give these forces direction by providing them with a philosophy and a principle of action: that of economic self-interest.

To Adam Smith himself this principle was not one of economic anarchy. For him "enlightened self-interest" was synonymous with a responsible concern for the common good. But it was the peculiar fatality of his viewpoint—and even of his phrasing—that it lent itself to misunderstanding and misapplication by immature minds. Whatever he may have intended, his philosophy became, in large measure, a rationalization by which men of driving energy and limited social understanding justified their concentrated pursuit of wealth and their reduction of their fellow men to the status of competitors, workers, and consumers.

It is interesting to note that those who turned Adam Smith's philosophy into a knife for cutting the bonds of mutual responsibility between man and man later found another tool for the same purpose in a misinterpretation of Darwin. By the time they had turned his scientific hypotheses into economic apologias, his phrase "the survival of the fittest" had come to signify that man proves his fitness by amassing wealth and running his competitors out of business. It had come to mean, also, that sympathy spent on victims of the economic struggle was sympathy wasted: such victims were Nature's unfit.

The concept of "economic man" not only pitted one individual against another, each absorbed in his own self-interest, but fostered yet another type of human fragmentation: it set one phase of man's nature against other phases. Economic advantage became something that could be pursued by means not subject to supervision by religion or ethics. Thus the life of the individual was divided into compartments, with such soundproof walls between them that a person in his role as "religious man," "civic man," or "domestic man" could not even hear what he said in his role as "economic man." Not only were men divided against themselves, but man was divided against himself.

One other nineteenth-century figure must be fitted into the company of those who thought the human race could prosper by a process of segmentation. With Hegel as his master, a poverty-stricken Jewish scholar sat, day after day, in the British Museum, searching through endless books to document a philosophic hunch. Karl Marx had been profoundly impressed by Hegel's formulation of all history as a struggle of opposites. Hegel had seen the struggle as one of ideas—a step by step working out of the logic of the World Spirit. Marx was fascinated by the clear-cut inevitability of the process. He felt that Hegel's analysis must be true: it was too convincingly neat to be false. Thesis—antithesis—synthesis; struggle of opposites—resolution of the struggle in a new synthesis—which itself became a new thesis; and so again, struggle, resolution of struggle. . . .

Marx accepted what seemed to him iron logic. This was what he had been looking for. He was facing the cruelties and confusions of nineteenth-century capitalism with burning indignation; he was intent to do more about these than merely to raise an outcry, as did the tenderhearted. He was set to undermine the whole system. Hegel pointed him the way. He took the logic that Hegel had applied to the world of abstract ideas and applied it to the hard realities of hunger and thirst, muscle and sweat, exploitation and profit-making.

Working in the British Museum, he piled up proofs of the chaos, the senselessness, the waste of human life that characterized the economic processes of his time. This was a job well done. No one had come within shouting distance of doing the job as he did it. Then he turned to the cure for the evil he depicted—and became, not a research scholar, but Hegel's disciple. The irrationality and immoralism of capitalistic practices would be superseded—why? Because man would grow wiser, surer in insight, more humane?—in brief, more mature? Not at all. Man's ideas and motives, mature or immature, were discarded as irrelevant. They had nothing to do with the issue. This was a business of cosmic dialectic at work in the economic sphere: class struggle would be the clue and the means to the world's advance. Here, again, we find the peculiar taint that marked so much of nineteenth-century thinking: here, again, we find one portion of the human race pitted against another and invited to an un-mitigated concentration upon its own advantage.

Nietzsche, Fichte, Hegel, Chamberlain, Adam Smith, Karl Marx—it would be hard to assemble a stranger company. What possible link could unite Nietzsche with Adam Smith; or Adam Smith with Karl Marx; or the Semitic Karl Marx with the fanatically anti-Semitic Chamberlain? Different as they all were, both in temperament and in the quality of their concern, these men yet belong together as contributors to the nineteenth-century mind: they all, in one way or another, re-pudiated or undermined doctrines that were favorable to maturity—the doctrines of social religion and political lib-eralism; they all, in one way or another, repudiated or under-mined the theory that the human race is one in destiny be-cause it is one in mutual need; they all took some selected portion of humanity—individual, nation, race, economic class —and urged it to become the triumphant protagonist in a drama of conflict in which some other portion of humanity was to be overcome. These voices were, in many respects, the dominating voices of the nineteenth century—and what they asked of man was something less than maturity; what they asked was that he become arrested at the level of individual or group egocentricity while, at the same time, he exercised every adult power he could command to gain his own ends.

IV

In yet another respect the philosophy that became peculiarly characteristic of the nineteenth century encouraged man to remain immature. Not only did it invite him, as we have seen, to egocentricity, but it invited him also to idealize the irrational.

To tabulate the major forms that antirationality took is to realize how far the mind of man had gone, in just a few decades, from the philosophy of eighteenth-century enlightenment: from the conviction that our rational capacities are equal to the solving of our personal and social problems.

For Nietzsche, the superman was in nowise the man who had, through the full use of his powers of understanding, transcended the ordinary limits of self and come to a comprehension of the whole. He was, instead, the man of force—and was exempted, by virtue of his strength, from the standards that smaller men must obey.

For Fichte, and other post-Kantian romantics, the ego was the arbiter of truth. With Fichte subjectivism became total and the human mind was left under no obligation to conform to any nonsubjective reality. Here was antirationalism of the first order—for it denied to man's rational powers any function worth performing.

For Schopenhauer, pessimist of the never-satisfied will, the wisdom of life was not to pit the rational mind against life's problems; the wisdom of life was to renounce all striving and to achieve a will-less oblivion.

For Hegel, the process by which the World Spirit operated was the dialectic one that we have already described. Thus Hegel presented to his century the dubious gift of "automatic progress": progress inherent in the logic of things and largely divorced from man's intentions and behaviors.

Adam Smith, by giving a strong philosophical push to man's scientific and economic energizing, encouraged the use of reason *within limits*. The technical and industrial advances that marked the nineteenth century were, in one sense, a tremendous monument to human reason. But rationality *in the part* did not, here, imply rationality *in the whole*. Instead, the doctrine of *laissez faire* set tacit limits to the area in which rationality might operate: rational man could and should, indeed, plan a research project, a machine, a business, an industry: but he must not plan a society.

Karl Marx similarly both affirmed and denied the use of reason. His own analysis of capitalistic offenses was a triumph of logic. His urgent demand that working men stop taking the economic order for granted was a bid for the increased use of the mind. But he, like Adam Smith, granted rationality only a *limited* utility: the process of social regeneration was to be that of conflict, not that of reason; and the classless society was to come without the members of one class ever using their minds to see inclusively the needs and problems of another class.

The widespread philosophizing of Darwinian biology introduced yet another form of antirationality: powers that distinguished man from other animals were played down; powers that proved him similar to them were played up; and as he was thus progressively converted into an animal fighting for survival, his claims to rationality were minimized and scorned.

Even Sigmund Freud, father of modern psychiatry, added his share to the conviction that man is irrational. The first effect of his studies of the human unconscious, as these studies penetrated the lay mind, was to make unreason seem far more exciting than reason. Being rational began to seem pretty dull stuff compared with being a creature in the grip of unconscious conflicts.

History sometimes does odd things with the works of men. Adam Smith, writing late in the eighteenth century, aimed to release human energies from arbitrary bonds; but the cumulative nineteenth-century effect of his work was to leave man trapped within a self-interest so narrowly defined that it had no use for many of his creative, rational, and empathic powers. Charles Darwin applied himself mightily to gain a rational view of the origin of species; but transmuted into pseudo-philosophy, his work encouraged men to deprecate their own powers of reason. Freud, who lived and wrote well into the twentieth century, voiced a conviction regarding man's irrationality that comported well with nineteenth-century attitudes. But psychiatrists who began as disciples of Freud have, by now, so modified his theories that they bid fair to become the leaders of a new movement toward rationality. What Freud began they have now carried on to a point where it seems apparent that man in the grip of irrational fears and hostilities is man defeated, and that our common aim must be to promote in our lives and institutions a mature rationality.

V

The nineteenth century *in its most characteristic developments* was the century of power politics and power economics: of aggressive nationalism, imperialism, trusts, "captains of industry," and "Napoleons of finance." These developments were all justified by the philosophies of the century: whether by the ego-centered, race-centered, and nation-centered romanticism of the Fichteans; the superman philosophy of the Nietzscheans; the "struggle for survival" philosophies of the various evolutionists; the cosmic dialectic of the Hegelians; the self-interest misinterpretations of Adam Smith's economics; or the dialectical materialism of the Marxians. Never, perhaps, in all history, has the madness of man's trying to go "too far alone" received such elaborate support; never, perhaps, has there been a more various rationalization of immaturity—or a more tragic handing over of authority to the mentally, emotionally, and socially immature.

A climate of opinion, like a physical climate, is so pervasive a thing that those who live within it and know no other take it for granted. We of the twentieth century—who still live, for the most part, in the nineteenth-century climate—are only beginning to be deeply troubled about a view of life which, in its intense competitiveness and consequent insecurity, has created what Karen Horney has called "the neurotic personality of our time": the isolated, fear-ridden, hostility-ridden personality; the personality, therefore, that is tenaciously immature.

It would be misleading to end our survey of the nineteenth century without some grateful reference to those who kept alive and carried on the philosophy of human worth and brotherhood. The century produced great figures and great movements; but the philosophies by which these figures and movements were animated were not in the main current of the century's thought-stream. Their activities were peripheral to the dominant activities that established the power-character of the period.

It is a truism that the nineteenth century produced great scientists. It is a fallacy, however, to say—as is commonly said—that it was therefore a scientific period. To have properly earned the adjective "scientific" it would have had to do precisely what it did not do: cultivate the scientific attitude toward all its problems and have habituated itself to the discipline of the scientific method. It would have had to set a premium upon objectivity instead of subjectivity; upon rationality instead of antirationality. The scientific attitude and method, elevated into the spirit of a century, would have made short shrift of the ego-centered posturings of supermen. What the great scientists of the century chiefly did was to remain outside the psychological, social, political, and economic problem-areas of their age. They went their independent way of research, leaving it to "practical men" to turn their discoveries into a "business civilization"; and leaving it to a dubious flock of pseudo-philosophers to turn their theories into justifications for ruthlessness.

The nineteenth century produced men of intellect who were also men of conscience. It produced John Stuart Mill, who grew beyond Bentham's "hedonistic calculus" and saw that a new world might be born from the industrial revolution if this revolution could be made to serve the interests of a genuine full-rounded individualism, not the narrowly conceived individualism that was rapidly supplanting the older humanistic concept. It produced Emerson, who had stout things to say about the growth of the individual into his proper human stature. It produced such men of the church as Channing, Wendell Phillips, and Theodore Parker; such men of the schools as Horace Mann, Francis Parker, and John Dewey; such men of philosophy as William James, Josiah Royce, and the lone Californian, George Holmes Howison; such men of the law as Holmes and Brandeis; such economists as J. A. Hobson, Simon Patten, and Thorstein Veblen; such businessmen as Robert Owen and David Lubin.

It produced the Fabian socialists who tried to work out a rational marriage of individualism and collectivism.

It produced the Rochdale weavers who, in the face of ridicule, wheeled their pathetic barrow of groceries down Toad Lane—and straight into the middle of the capitalistic system—stubbornly setting it down there and initiating the consumers' co-operatives.

The century produced utopians; and off-the-line figures like William Morris, John Ruskin, and Thoreau; humorists like Mark Twain and Peter Finley Dunne; anti-imperialists like the poet William Vaughn Moody; journalists like Lincoln Steffens and Ida Tarbell; antimilitarists like Stephen Crane;

revolutionists like Prince Kropotkin, with his theory of mutual aid.

Most characteristically of all, perhaps, the century produced great alleviators: men and women of mind and conscience who set themselves to rescue the victims of industrial exploitation. The names of such individuals as Charles Kingsley, Jane Addams, and Lillian Wald, give pride to those who set a high premium on emotional and social maturity. Accurate knowledge, a sense of creative responsibility, empathy, and a philosophy that stressed the oneness of mankind—these qualities marked, in pre-eminent degree, those who, in the darkening decades of man's ruthlessness to man, set themselves to the hard task of defending the helpless, the exploited, the discards on the human scrap heap.

The nineteenth century, in brief, produced its measure of mature men and women; but these men and women were not permitted to shape the dominant institutions of the period. Instead, they had to hold their own against those dominant institutions. They were the living heirs to the tradition of liberalism and enlightenment; but the status of that tradition had been so reduced in the late nineteenth century that it was typified by the alleviative settlement house, whereas in the late eighteenth century, its accomplishment was the American Bill of Rights.

VI

What we have tried to sum up in this chapter is the fact that our culture is marked, not by inner consistency, but by raw conflicts. These conflicts have produced certain common effects that are clearly relevant to our problem of maturity.

First, the typical member of our culture is, by now, a *divided self*: a prey to doubts, fears, and inner tensions that express themselves in forms as various as alcoholism and anti-Semitism; apathy and driving ambition; faith in education and contempt for educated people. Where, in brief, there is a lack of *wholeness* within the conditioning influences brought to bear upon the individual, the individual is not likely to be whole, or psychologically mature.

Second, the typical member of our culture is a *compartmentalized self*. He effects a spurious inner harmony by parceling out to competing philosophies the various phases of his own experience—so that the domestic self, the business self, the religious self, the political self, the convention-attending self, and all the others, are housed in one body but remain as much strangers to one another as do the residents of an urban apartment house. Every psychiatrist can testify that the modern individual makes tragic and futile efforts to achieve peace within himself by becoming a veritable crowd of different compartmentalized selves.

Third, it has become extraordinarily difficult in our twentieth century for the human being to grow out of psychological childhood into maturity. With the natural hazards of life vastly multiplied by the confusions of his culture, he faces an abnormal temptation to remain dependent and irresponsible. It is never easy, even at the best, for the individual to build sound knowledge linkages with his world; but it becomes infinitely difficult for him to do so in a cultural atmosphere where education is both exalted and despised; where the same two parents send him to school, want him to bring home grades they can view with pride, talk about the impracticality of what is learned in school, admire people less for what they know than for what they own, and make it clear that teachers are nobodies compared with businessmen and movie stars. Again, it is never easy for an individual to build sound responsibility linkages; but it becomes more than difficult in a cultural atmosphere where the Sabbath-day avowal of the brotherhood of man is contradicted by the week-day fight for his own survival and enrichment. Confusion of values makes for a sense of personal bewilderment and helplessness; and the average individual of our century gets what happiness he can out of doing what everybody does. To accept the going standards—as a child accepts the word of the parent—becomes the "survival" wisdom of our day.

Fourth, those philosophies that ask a high level of maturity command a smaller following than do those that accept adult immaturity as good enough. As we have seen, one major strain in our tradition—that of intellectual and social liberalism—urges us to grow up into our full psychological stature. This tradition is rendered all the lip-service it could ask, but little enough behavior-service. For among the philosophies that compete with it are at least two that demand less effort and give quicker rewards: the strain of religious and political authoritarianism, and the strain of materialism and antirationalism. Each of these presents a much easier way of life than the philosophy that asks us to make efforts to grow up.

Fifth, the inherent confusion brought about by the competition of philosophies is further compounded by strange alliances among them. It is notorious, for example, that more ministers lined up, during the nineteenth century, with the owners of factories and tenements than with those who sought to curb the exploitative power of those owners. Their Bible urged them to feed the hungry and clothe the naked; but their basic definition of man as a child of sin made them set so high a premium upon obedience, on the one hand, and the exercise of authority on the other, that their whole character structure bade them support those in power against those who questioned the rightness of power. Authoritative religion might want man to remain a child in his obedience and dependence, while nineteenth-century antirationalism might want him to remain a child in egocentric self-aggrandizement; but in an emergency, the two would accurately feel that they had more in common than either had with a philosophy that asked man to put his childhood behind him and to achieve the spiritual independence of maturity.

Sixth, the typical member of our culture can express the highest idealism and practice the crassest "realism" without ever knowing that the two are in contradiction. Political speakers repeat great phrases of Thomas Jefferson, or George Washington, or Woodrow Wilson—honestly believing them; and then make shady political deals; businessmen quote Abraham Lincoln and then lobby to prevent slum clearance; the average citizen expresses pride in the American Bill of Rights, and then seeks to protect his real estate by restrictive covenants. Socrates, with his keen power to detect inner contradictions and bring them to light would have had an Athenian holiday among the men and women of our century. What our century would do to him, we leave to conjecture.

Finally, all the major institutions of our society are—like individuals—divided selves rather than whole selves. The influence they exert upon individuals is therefore never one that makes for a confident and productive wholeness of character.

It is with these signs of inner contradiction in mind that we close our present chapter and turn to the chapters that lie ahead. In them we shall examine some of the chief institutions that shape our individual and our common lives. We shall try to measure their fitness for that task by asking *to what extent they embody and encourage maturing, and to what extent they embody and encourage fixation in immaturity.* Only when we have made such an analysis can we be intelligent enough to know what to do about institutions that make us what we are, and that we, in at least some measure, are privileged and obligated to remake.

SIX

APPLIED MATURITY: A TEST CASE

MATURITY is always, in one way or another, *maturity at work*. This is true in our intimate personal relationships. It is true no less in our relationship to institutions and to such movements of the public mind as bring new institutions to birth.

In order to see how mature or immature we now commonly are, we can do no better than to size up what our reaction as an American people has been to the central problem of our time: that of moving out of provincialism into One World. Each age, it seems, puts its own peculiar test to the human race; asks man whether or not he can achieve the mental, emotional, and social stature requisite to the solving of some key problem or cluster of problems. There can be little doubt that the key problem of our period is that of expressing through adequate political and legal institutions the oneness of the human race.

This problem, at the moment of writing, poses two urgent questions: what to do about the atomic bomb; and what to do about Russia. Here is something more than material for newspaper headlines. These are specific challenges to our character structure; specific tests of our maturity. If we have, so far, shown ourselves fairly mature in our responses to these particular problems, then we have a right to assume that our major institutions have, on the whole, fostered maturity in us—and a right, therefore, to assume that we will be able to handle future problems as these may arise. If, on the other hand, examination shows that our responses have been conspicuously immature—uninformed, biased, shortsighted, irresponsible, naïve, self-centered, apathetic—then we must assume that something in our institutions has encouraged us to remain immature.

I I

The psychological chain reaction that was set going when the atomic bomb fell on Hiroshima will not expend itself until it has in some degree influenced the fate of every man, woman, and child on the planet—or yet to be born on the planet. It is as though, in the moment of that bomb's explosion, a problem that had sprawled through the ages was brought to sharp focus: can men and nations resolve their mutual disagreements and misunderstandings without recourse to such orgies of mutual killing that the final result is racial suicide?

In the fall of 1945, atomic energy was front page news. No scientific discovery was ever so dramatically introduced. Within a few months more Americans had heard of the atomic bomb than had heard of the United Nations, and technical words of the physicist had become part of the daily vocabulary. It was generally recognized that this discovery had created new problems. But what the problems are; indeed, what are the important facts still remain a mystery to most citizens. Atomic energy is being used by isolationists to prove that the U.S. is impregnable and by internationalists to prove that world government is mandatory. One group argues that it makes armies obsolete and another concludes that it makes peacetime conscription imperative. The facts are not abstruse, the implications are not obscure, and both are vitally related to the decisions which citizens must make.[1]

That there is wide disagreement should not be surprising. Something new under the sun has been created, and we as citizens do not as yet know what to do with this new thing. What interests us here, however, is the question of how the American mind has, in general, reacted to this new thing which presents so great a danger not only to the personal survival of every one of us but to the survival of civilization. Have Americans, by and large, responded to the problem of atomic energy with a solicitude commensurate with the significance of that problem? Have they set themselves resolutely and responsibly to learn such facts as can be learned and make such rational deductions as can be made? Have they shown a mature imagination about what actually happened at Hiroshima and in subsequent tests of the atomic

[1] W. A. Higinbotham, "Foreword by an Atomic Scientist," in *The Journal of Social Issues*, Vol. IV, No. 1, Winter 1948, p. 2.

bomb? Have they come together in groups to think over and talk over the monstrous event that has taken place? Have they proved their awareness of what is at stake by making it unmistakably clear to their representatives in government that they will not tolerate the application of old narrow partisanships to the new broad problem of atomic energy?

More than two years have now passed since the atomic bomb moved out of the laboratory into the headlines; out of the area of rumor into the area of fact. Have Americans made up their minds about its future use and control? Have they seriously tried to make up their minds?

> Findings of public opinion surveys indicate that a large part of the American public lacks the information which would be necessary for them to understand even the broadest aspects of the decisions the nations must make on foreign policy. Furthermore, there is a widespread tendency for people to avoid thinking about international problems, on the grounds that they are too complex or too frightening.[2]

In the report of the results of a study made by the Survey Research Center of the University of Michigan, Patricia Woodward writes:

> First of all there can be no doubt as to the tremendous impact which the atomic bomb had on the minds of the American people. All but one or two persons out of every hundred had heard of the atomic bomb and understood that an extraordinary event had occurred . . .

[2] *Journal of Social Issues,* Winter 1948, p. 5.

Beyond this concept of the bomb as extremely dangerous and destructive, however, agreement ceased. One might expect such a belief to lead automatically to an active concern about the bomb . . . the problem of its control and the possibility of its use in war. This does not seem to be the case. Even one year after the startling announcement of the bomb, public thinking about it could not be described as 'active concern.' And now, more than two years after Hiroshima, there is not any evidence that the concern has increased . . .

The general lack of active concern—indeed, near apathy toward the bomb—seems to stem primarily from a feeling of helplessness, a belief that there is little or nothing the individual can do about the problem . . .

This is the upshot of the report: a general feeling of helplessness; therefore, a general tendency to push the whole problem out of mind. Even the relatively well-informed about world affairs "were as likely as the poorer-informed to say they were not at all worried about the atomic bomb because 'worry is useless.' " [3]

These conclusions have a profound *political* significance: they seem to indicate that the problem of atomic energy will be handled in accordance with pre-atomic practices of diplomacy, with a minimum of attention to the hopes and fears of the general mass of people whose lives are at issue. But the conclusions have, as well, a profound *psychological* significance. A feeling of helplessness in the face of a problem basic

[3] "How Do the American People Feel about the Atomic Bomb?" in *Journal of Social Issues*, Vol. IV, No. 1, p. 7.

to life is not the sign of a mind in mature command of itself. It is the sign of a mind that has given up. Theoretically, Americans have had, by now, more opportunity and longer opportunity than any other people on earth to get hold of such facts as they think they need for the solution of their problems. They enjoy a maximum chance both to do individual research, when they feel themselves unequipped with the materials with which to think about an issue, and to get together in groups to pool information and to probe their differences of opinion. Theoretically, also, they have long been conditioned to the philosophy that "governments derive their just powers from the consent of the governed"; and they have had a long chance to learn how to make their citizen-influence felt. What is it, then, that makes Americans feel so helpless in the face of the problem of atomic energy that they are ready to abdicate from their role of responsible citizens and think about something else? Is their feeling of helplessness peculiar to this case—perhaps because they have confused the knowledge necessary for making an atomic bomb with the attitudes necessary for its social control? Or is the feeling of helplessness symptomatic? Does it extend widely to other areas of social and political concern? If so, what does it tell about the level of our psychological maturity—and about what must be done to raise that level?

III

We turn, now, to the second problem that we have chosen as a key problem: what to do about Russia. In a report on

The American Concept of Russia, undertaken by this same Survey Research Center of the University of Michigan, Angus Campbell writes:

> Public attitudes toward the Soviet Union develop within the context of beliefs, values, and information within which the American people appraise all phases of international affairs.[4]

Another way to say this would be that, confronted by the problem of our future relationship with Russia, we respond less in terms of the objective character of the problem than in terms of our own character structures. What, precisely, is our "context of beliefs, values, and information" that operates in this case? When we take the answers given by the survey, and lay against those answers our yardstick of psychological maturity, the results are singularly revealing:

> It is clear, for example, that Americans generally regard their country as fair and just in relation to other countries. Relatively few people are inclined to cynical analysis of this country's motivation in its past or present dealings with other nations. The public generally accept the supposition that this country is 'honorable' in its activities on the international scene and they tend to assume that the peoples of the world recognize this fact. They compare the behavior of other countries unfavorably in this regard.

If this is a true report on our prevailing attitude, as it would seem to be, it follows that our appraisal of any international

4 "The American Concept of Russia," in *Journal of Social Issues,* Vol. IV, No. 1, p. 15.

disagreement in which our country is involved will be an appraisal that is slanted *even before any facts are examined.* We might put the matter in terms of a logical syllogism. If the major premise that we bring to all thinking about international problems is that our country is 'honorable' and that other countries compare unfavorably with it in this respect, then our conclusion in a specific case will not be independent of that major premise. In any given international disagreement—as in our present disagreement with Russia—our country may be in the right; or partially in the right and partially in the wrong. But the *degree* of our rightness would, by mature standards, have to be determined by an objective analysis of motives and maneuvers; not by a fixed-in-advance attitude of the we-are-good-and-you-are-not-so-good variety. Such a fixed-in-advance attitude is a child's attitude: "My family is better than your family"; "My father is stronger than your father." It is an attitude bred by the need to feel secure in a situation when one is not yet maturely in command of one's own powers.

The report continues:

> Americans are particularly strong in the conviction that their country is a non-aggressive, peaceful nation. They take it for granted that their country has no territorial ambitions which it wishes to impose on other countries. They assume that this country would undertake hostile action against another country only as a means of defense.

In any given case, we must again emphasize, such confidence in our country's motives may be justified; but an assumption

to that effect *that precedes an examination of the evidence*
is not a mature tribute of respect to a country that has proudly
proclaimed its citizens capable of self-government and ready
for participation in world affairs. It is rather like the naïvely
loaded statement with which I once heard a minister open
a young people's discussion group: "Tonight we are going
to have a free, fair, and honest discussion of all the world's
major religions and show why Christianity is the best."

The preconceptions that Americans bring to their thinking
about world affairs do not, as the report testifies, prevent their
bringing good intentions:

> The American public is anxious to safeguard world peace and
> feels that this country should take part in international con-
> ferences devoted to this objective. In the abstract, the concept
> of international cooperation is an attractive one to most Ameri-
> cans but they do not characteristically have any detailed plan
> for the implementation of such a policy.

A belief that America operates on a higher ethical plane than
other nations no more contradicts a hope for One World than
a zealous missionary belief in the superiority of one's own
religion contradicts a hope that all mankind may eventually
be saved *through an acceptance of that religion.* Americans,
in brief, are emotionally ready to move out of national provincialism *on their own terms;* ready to welcome a form of
internationalism that will be their own form of provincialism
writ large. This is not, in terms of psychological maturity, the
same thing as being ready for a genuine internationalism.

The hopes that many Americans voice for world peace and

world unity have about them in fact much of the quality of childish and adolescent daydreams in which the "right" person is always the hero and in which results are achieved without much regard for cause and effect.

The general and specific attitudes which Americans hold regarding world problems very often have the most meager informational content. Information regarding world affairs is highly concentrated within the small fraction of the population of this country who keep themselves well-informed. The few who know in detail the facts of contemporary affairs are greatly outnumbered by the many who have only a smattering of information on these subjects. The general level of enlightenment may be judged from the fact that one adult in three is still unable after two years of tremendous publicity regarding the United Nations to indicate any understanding of what that organization is set up to do. Since nearly the entire population has either newspapers or radio regularly available in their homes it must be concluded that public ignorance in this field is very much more the result of public apathy than it is of any difficulty in obtaining the facts . . .

The issue of Communism is highly confused in the minds of most Americans. While a vague connection is made between Communism and Russians, only a small minority of the people understand in any detail the ideology of Communism . . . Many people have very elementary notions regarding American Communists, tending to identify as Communist any belligerent non-conformist, i.e., John L. Lewis . . .

Generally speaking, the American people seem well satisfied with the behavior of their Government in its relations to the Soviet Union . . . The reason that these people most commonly give for their satisfaction is the belief that this country has been 'fair' in its dealings with the Soviet Union . . .

For a large proportion of the public, attitudes toward Russia are based on vague, general impressions rather than specific information regarding particular issues or events . . .

IV

It might be said, of course, that this survey has disclosed nothing new: that we have known all along that most Americans are too vague about the specific details of either domestic or foreign affairs to make informed judgments. The very fact, however, that we so readily shrug off our ignorance—as something to be expected and not taken too seriously—is in itself a significant comment upon us. If we were British, we might speak with affection and pride of our historic success in muddling through. Being Americans, we rely on our feeling that things will somehow come out all right. It is this national optimism, divorced alike from logic and specific knowledge, that Arthur Guiterman parodied in his brief poem, "Prayer":

> Providence, that watches over children, drunkards, and fools
> With silent miracles and other esoterica,
> Continue to suspend the ordinary rules
> And take care of the United States of America! [5]

Ours is—or for a long time, was—a pleasant optimism, happily compounded out of physical exuberance; space in which

[5] Copyright 1933, The New Yorker Magazine, Inc. Included in the volume *Gaily the Troubador*, published by E. P. Dutton & Co., Inc.

to move; technological advances; faith in mankind; evidence that other countries identified progress with becoming more like us in both government and industry; trust in Providence; a non-statistical conviction that people get pretty much what they deserve; and a peculiarly durable hope on the part of the average individual that his ship would somehow come in, whether or not he could point to any time and place where it had been launched.

The limitations of such optimism—and the immaturity of it—are now becoming ever more apparent. They are made apparent by the readiness with which we slip into a feeling of helplessness when we are confronted by a problem that does not yield to ready solution. They are made apparent, likewise, by our quick retreat from such a complex problem into "not worrying because it won't do any good." Our optimism, in brief, has the curious effect of paralyzing our sense of responsibility and our powers of reason rather than of releasing them. It makes us more ready to let events take their course—even if that course be potentially disastrous to ourselves and to those we love—than to exert ourselves to direct those events.

Our policy of drift, where our human future is concerned, has, to be sure, been punctuated by brief periods of concentrated effort. At the time of the Dumbarton Oaks proposals, for example, we rallied nationwide to study and discuss. All over the country, study groups were formed, meetings were held, resolutions were passed. We showed ourselves determined to create a new kind of world. Through the sustained

pressure of our public opinion we persuaded a hitherto un-
decided or reluctant Congress to the creation of the United
Nations. We had, it seemed, grown up abruptly to a mature
realization of our responsibility. Then the signs of immaturity
began to show.

In the first place, we were unable to sustain interest in the
new world thus created. As though the United Nations
organization was merely a sort of nine days' wonder from
which attention could be withdrawn with impunity when
boredom set in, we turned back to our own affairs—or to
whatever was new in the headlines. When the United Nations was no longer a "cause" in behalf of which we could
get up meetings and stage parades; when it was a working
organization busy with the wearisome task of ironing out
international differences, we got bored and impatient . . .
and let our minds wander . . .

In the second place, we found it well-nigh impossible to
accept the sphere of international affairs as one of give and
take. We carried into our appraisal of the United Nations
all our fixed nationalism—so that we felt that if our country
yielded on any point, it was proving itself weak, while if other
nations refused to yield, they were proving themselves stubborn. In short, though we talked of one world, we thought in
terms of winning and losing.

In the third place, we slipped back with shocking ease into
the old conviction that when there are deep cleavages between nations the thing to do is to start frightening one another instead of understanding one another.

V

Psychologically speaking, our American history is difficult to appraise with any degree of fairness. Our nation was born under the aegis of a philosophy that actually invited man to grow up. That philosophy was not then, nor has it been before or since, the dominant world philosophy. For a few creative decades, however, it was strong enough in a few places—as on the North American continent—to challenge old authoritarian systems and to write its own documents of freedom. Such documents not only repudiated various older philosophies, but they were far ahead of the practices of even those who were to live under them—so far ahead, indeed, that those who were to live under them were almost inevitably destined in some measure to fail. All estimates of the American story and of current American behavior must take this fact into account.

Again, it is extremely difficult, in telling our American story and appraising our behavior, to know how much weight to give to our native psychological traits and how much to the circumstances that have surrounded our national growth. In practice, these have become indiscriminately combined.

The material resources at our command, for example, have had a varied effect upon our character structure and history. Without these resources, the colonists would scarcely have developed that conviction regarding their own capabilities that made them ready for independence. Hence the first effect of these resources must be counted as a maturing one: through them, to an almost unprecedented degree, plain men learned what powers in themselves they could rely upon.

These resources, moreover, gave us time to learn our initial lessons in republicanism without coming a complete cropper. They enabled us to hold our own against European monarchies that wanted our experiment to fail. Also, they allowed us a wide margin for non-tragic error. Thus, we could discover that the Articles of Confederation would not work, and could move ahead from these to the drawing up of a Constitution instead of moving back from them to our pre-Revolutionary state of dependence. Many European experiments in democracy have, we know, failed precisely because they have enjoyed no such margin for error.

These resources have been responsible, likewise, for our vast material expansion and for the scientific and technological ingenuity to which they have given an outlet. Our scientific and technological powers have matured, not only because they have been part of our native equipment, but because they have had materials to work with.

On other counts, however, our natural resources have kept us immature. They have, all too often, made us take credit to ourselves not only for what we have earned by ingenuity and effort but for what we were given by nature. Thus, self-deceived about our own accomplishments, we have too often felt fully able to give advice to nations struggling along on a far lower level of resources. Again, our natural riches long made it possible for men to succeed on the frontier, or as exploiters of forests and mines, without a mature imagination about other people or a mature skill in the arts of community. Once more, our resources have tempted us to a one-sided development: to an overemphasis upon material goods. Finally, our resources have so long allowed us to be wasteful —like adolescents supported by wealthy and indulgent parents—that when we have to begin to show some such prudence as most of the human race has always had to show, we incline toward an immature bitterness rather than toward a mature marshaling of our powers. It is never easy for those who have enjoyed making the gestures of the spendthrift to undertake the husbanding of limited resources.

Not only the native endowment of our continent, but other factors as well have operated to shape an American character structure that is a blend of the mature and the immature. The fact, for example, that all our history has lain within a period of rapid change has had its effect upon us. On the one hand, it has made for flexibility of mind; readiness for the new. It has made the burden of outworn tradition a light load upon our shoulders—a far lighter load than most peoples have had to carry. On the other hand, it has discouraged us from setting a proper value upon the virtue of patience: what cannot be quickly done seems to us scarcely worth doing. Also—combined with the presence of such contradictory philosophies as we examined in the preceding chapter—it has made it hard for us to achieve any stability of standards; any personal or group habit of measuring our actual behaviors against permanent principles of behavior. Finally, it has kept us, in many respects, so overstimulated that our responses are surface-responses. A child, we now know, is likely to be halted in its growth toward psychological maturity if it is subjected to too many stimuli that call for an immediate reaction, and if it is given too little leisure and privacy in which to assimilate what it has experienced. It is simply not good for a child to have too many toys, so that it never has time deeply to love one; or to be too constantly surrounded by people; or to be too constantly on the go; or to have so many activities organized for it that it never has time just to be itself in a kind of divine idleness. The process of psychological maturing is more than the process of receiving impressions, one after another. It is the process of savoring these impressions until they yield up their meaning. It is the process of letting new experiences turn around and around in the mind until they find the angle at which they want to settle down among old experiences. We as a people are, in many respects, like children who have been exposed to too many changing stimuli in too rapid a succession: we are both excitable and emotionally fatigued; both ready for the new, whatever it is, and unready for any of its meanings that are not on the surface: both ego-centered wanters of more and more and generous givers of what we have—less in the spirit of those who will divide their last crust than in the spirit of those who feel that they will soon have something better to take the place of what they give away.

VI

This quick survey of our American history and character may seem to have little application to the original question that we set out to explore: the question of how mature or immature we are showing ourselves to be with reference to the key problem of our age—that of building one world. But the seeming irrelevance covers a deep relevancy. For the character structure that we have built in the past is the character structure that we now have to work with—and that we are now variously revealing.

One trait with which most Americans will credit themselves is independence. They claim it for their individual selves, and they claim it for their nation. They are not, so they say, going to let anybody push them around. They don't need anybody to tell them what to think. If so-and-so doesn't like what they do, he can go jump in the lake—and the so-and-so may be a neighbor or a fellow nation. They can stand on their own feet; look after themselves; work their own way up—and they expect others to do the same. God helps those who help themselves.

For the average American, in brief, the word *independence* is always, in large measure, a fighting word. It has less to do with the full development of the unique self than with the capacity to resist pressures, to overcome obstacles, to tell the other person off, to go it alone. That it should have this definition is not strange in the light of our history. As a nation, we had to make a place for ourselves in a hostile and sneering world; and during eventful decades, when we had not yet proved ourselves—when our democratic experiment was still in the balance—we learned self-defensively to "tell off" the rest of the world. Moreover, both frontier conditions and nineteenth-century philosophy encouraged us to spell the word *independence* with a capital I, encouraged us to minimize the arts of community and to play up the ego as the all-triumphant.

This is the concept of independence that we bring with us now into the council of nations. It has, in many respects, served us well in the past—when we had to go it alone or perish. We are enormously proud of it—having made it the key to our personal and national significance. Yet it is not a mature concept. It writes the ego too large; it has little patience with the slow processes of mutual understanding; it is far too weak an invitation to empathy; it militates against *whole*-seeing; it makes us ready, as we have already seen, to regard it as a defeat if our nation yields on any point in disagreement with another nation.

All too often we have seen how an immature definition of *independence* can stunt the psychological development. The boy who is forced to work his way while he should be still a secure resident of home and school easily learns to think in terms of struggle, not in terms of mutual understanding. If he achieves material success, he is apt not only to take full credit for it but to be contemptuous of those who remain dependent longer than he did or who incline toward co-operative ventures. Also, he tends to carry a once-useful belligerence into situations where it is actually a handicap. It becomes a testimony, then, not to his possession of genuine strength but, rather, to his long having had to make his weakness into premature strength, his young fear into a premature self-confidence, and his immaturity into a show of maturity. Now that he is an adult, he may have kindly impulses and the best of intentions; but instead of being the man of such tried inner confidence that he does not have to be always proving himself, he is likely to be the man of power who throws his weight around. There is some danger that we Americans, now that our nation is the richest on earth, may find ourselves in the grip of a similar immaturity—a similar belligerent conception of the word *independence*.

Closely related to this attitude of self-defensive belligerence is the common tendency to compare ourselves with other peoples to their disadvantage. The habitual retort, for example, to any statement about the poverty in our own midst is that we have the highest standard of living in the world. Here again the clue is to be found in psychological immaturity. One mark of maturity is the power to think in terms of principles and *the willingness to have one's own behavior measured by those principles*. It is the self-excusing child, not the man of mature self-respect, who says, "Well, I don't care . . . I got a better grade than John did" or "I don't see why *I* have to do my chores. Bill didn't do his." Americans, at the outset of their national career, laid down some notable principles relative to human rights and relationships. To the extent that they individually and collectively measure themselves by these, they become mature. To the extent that they count it a legitimate self-excuse that other individuals or nations are not as good as they are, they tend to fixate themselves in immaturity.

We have already taken brief stock of two other characteristics that are showing up in our attitudes toward the one world problem: our tendency to exhibit an interest and then let it dwindle; and our widespread feeling of helplessness— with the consequent tendency to push out of mind a problem that baffles us.

The former—the inability to sustain an interest until a task is completed—is unmistakably a childish trait. It belongs legitimately to the time of life when the immediate moment is still the only real moment and when the sense of long-range cause and effect is rudimentary. Obviously, this is a time when the child is not carrying any major responsibility. He is still a dependent. If the individual—or the nation—takes on responsibility without acquiring the power to sustain an interest, the condition must be rated as one of arrested development. From a psychological angle, it seems likely that the contrast between our initial interest in the United Nations and our later boredom with it is but part and parcel of a larger immaturity: an immaturity bred of the overstimulation we have already analyzed. A national habit of responding to immediate sense data in a world of rapid change is not a habit conducive to the solid sustaining of interest when a matter of real moment is at stake.

The feeling of helplessness is likewise a mark of immaturity. It means that in spite of all our vaunted independence, we are accustomed to having some authority speak the word. When we are confronted by a problem that we cannot solve by simply taking sides, a problem that leaves "authorities" divided among themselves, we do not know what to do. We find that our actual experience in citizenship has rarely involved us in a serious weighing of issues; even more rarely has it involved us in research. We have played our game of self-government according to the rules of party loyalties; we have "made up our own minds" by choosing which authority to quote. When this method fails us—as it has where the atomic bomb is concerned—we feel lost. Then, for the political or journalistic authority who has let us down, we substitute a cosmic authority, a parental providence: we decide not to worry, because everything will come out all right, somehow . . . and anyway, we can't do anything about it . . .

What we have said in this chapter may seem an unfair judgment on our American behavior. In many respects, we are a far more mature people than we were even a generation ago. War and depression have humbled us into a kind of maturity. We are not so sure as we once were that providence regards us as a special case. We are not so sure that we have all the answers. Yet the old immaturities linger on. So many of them linger on, in fact, that we stand in grave danger of having even our new humility go to waste: in rescuing us from cocky childishness, it may land us merely in a submissive childishness; it may merely send us looking for some new authoritative "parent" on whom we can rely.

The old immaturities linger on—to make us inept in a new role where maturity is called for. The fact that they thus linger on invites us to look with questioning eyes at the practices and institutions that have made us what we are.

SEVEN

ECONOMICS FOR HUMAN FULFILLMENT

IN THE TIME of Aristotle, the word *oikonomike* meant "the management of the household." Economics had to do with an over-all concern for group well-being. It was a science, therefore, that dealt with the relation of goods to needs, the aim being a smooth-running household unit.

By the nineteenth century, this view of economics had practically disappeared. Adam Smith tried to keep it alive by his conception of the "wealth of nations," in which he visualized the nation as a sort of household writ large. But a century booming ahead with steam machinery and colonial exploitation would have none of it. As we have already seen, that century took from Adam Smith only what fitted its own purposes. The most dramatic single effect, perhaps, of the coming of industrialism was to shift the emphasis from *goods for use* to *goods for sale:* from consumption to production. "Wealth" came less and less to imply the possession of means by which to satisfy both needs and tastes, and came more and more to imply the possession of a money surplus beyond all possible utility—a surplus to be used to build up a further surplus, and to be enjoyed as power.

British economists, knowing from their college Greek the "household" meaning of economics, and aware of the contradiction between that meaning and the science they themselves were creating, tried to substitute a more accurately descriptive term. Whately suggested *catallactics,* the science of exchanges. The economics of his day, he felt, far from being concerned about the members of a household, was concerned about "trading." It was the practice of giving *quid pro quo*—and of being shrewd enough to see to it that the *quid* one received was somewhat greater than the *quo* one gave. Hearn suggested *plutology,* the science of wealth— meaning, in nineteenth-century terms, not the group-wealth upon which all the members of a household or a society could draw, but the wealth that an individual could gain and control. Ingram was the bluntest of all. He suggested *chrematistics,* the science of money-making. These efforts to reform the language in the service of accuracy came to nothing. The word *economics* kept its hold on the tongues of men. But it became, so to speak, merely a container out of which one meaning had been taken and into which another meaning had been put: it no longer had any logical relationship to the use men made of it.

It is a long psychological road from the "management of a

household," or even the "wealth of nations," to "money-making." Yet this is the long road that our civilization has traveled—and in the process of traveling it, men have, in large measure, developed a different character structure. They have learned to attach importance to different phases of their own nature; to laud as commendable different habits and attitudes; to strive for approval and prestige by different means; to see themselves as differently related to other members of the human group; to have different ambitions, different fears, and a different conception of success and failure. They have become, in brief, not members of a household so much as members of a "business civilization"—a money-making civilization.

We know what the change has meant in material terms. The laudatory phrases have come tumbling from speeches and books. Never in all history has the physical standard of living risen so fast and so high as in those countries animated by the industrial revolution and the economics of capitalism. Never have goods been produced in such plenty; never have inventions multiplied so brilliantly; never have so many ills— of inconvenience, discomfort, and disease—been dispelled for so many people. The making of money, in short, has meant the making of an unprecedented material "prosperity"—for that portion of the planet where the money has been made. It has meant the building of a civilization better equipped with more tools for doing more things rapidly and accurately than any civilization that ever existed before. "Money-making," in a material sense, has unquestionably produced not only many goods, but also much good. When we turn to its psychological influence, however, we are forced to ask whether what it has produced is good enough—or is logically on the way to becoming good enough.

I I

A psychological report on our "business" civilization is far harder to draw up than is a material report. We no sooner venture our analysis than we find ourselves in a complex welter of pros and cons, and of half-truths that must be carefully qualified if they are to serve as whole truths.

How difficult our problem is may become evident if we will think, for a moment, of some of those basic linkages with life that we have already defined as essential to our maturing.

Thus, there is the *knowledge linkage*. Man matures, we have noted, to the extent that he gains knowledge enough to handle with competent understanding the situation in which he finds himself; and to the extent, also, that he has the habits and means of gaining further knowledge as his situation changes. That situation may change, as we know, for two reasons: either because he has grown up to a new level of responsibility—as parent, wage earner, or voting citizen; or because his material and cultural environment has undergone some significant shift.

In terms of this one linkage—the *knowledge linkage*—how shall we rate the effect of industrial capitalism upon the human race? On the one hand, obviously, it has greatly increased the spread of knowledge: of books, newspapers, radio programs, and all the rest. It has multiplied schools, colleges, and institutions of adult education. It has meant the enormous

development of what we might call "the art of convention"—
the coming together of specialists of like interest to pool their
information and experience. More facts have been set at large
within the human scene than ever before in human history;
and because the dissemination of facts has been made into a
source of profit, efforts to channel knowledge into minds have
been intense and ingenious. One vastly encouraging result of
all this has been that area after area of human experience has
been rescued from the tyranny of superstition, rule-of-thumb
folklore, and sheer helpless ignorance. In this respect, there
can be no doubt whatever about the increased competence,
and therefore the increased maturity, of the common mind.

On the other hand, it may well be doubted whether the
average member of our business civilization *feels* more competent, *feels* more adept at handling his life, *feels* more confident of his hold upon necessary facts than did his pre-
industrial forebears. Psychological maturity, with respect to
the *knowledge linkage,* has less to do with how many facts
and skills are at command than with *a relationship between
facts known and situation to be handled.* We have noted in
the preceding chapter that modern man is commonly marked
by a sense of helplessness in political matters; not by a sense
of adequacy. Other areas of his life—the vocational area, for
example—are similarly pervaded by a sense of helplessness.
If we ask why the spread of knowledge that has undoubtedly
accompanied the spread of industrialism has brought with it
a widespread loss of self-confidence, we may note three major
reasons. First, the number of things that modern man would
have to know in order actually to understand his situation has

increased far more rapidly than the number of things he does know—so that the balance has been weighted *against* his feeling himself equal to what life demands. Secondly, the spread of knowledge by industrial processes has made less for the independence of the individual than for his dependence: a smaller and smaller proportion of the things that he knows can be checked by his actual experience, and a larger and larger proportion of them have to be taken on authority; also, fewer and fewer of the facts that he knows have any relationship to his own capacity to satisfy his own basic needs by his own efforts. He may distinguish himself on a quiz program; but he does not know how, except by the indirect and precarious means of money-making, to provide himself with food and shelter. Third, since industrial capitalism has turned knowledge into a commodity to be sold on the market—and to be sold, therefore, like shoes or thumb tacks, to as many people as possible—the standard under which it is produced and distributed is less that of accuracy and human utility than that of attractiveness. It is not surprising, under these conditions, that information and misinformation reach the public in an undifferentiated mass; that the facts marketed are those that the seller thinks will be most popular with most buyers—as when scandal is marketed in the headlines; and that the "facts" are often not facts at all, but merely a reflection of what some special interest group would find it profitable to have the public accept. Shall we say, then, that industrialism has been a force for maturity because it has made more people "better informed"? Or shall we say that it has been a force for immaturity because it has made more people self-convicted of ignorance and helplessness—and has encouraged them, therefore, to a lifelong dependence in the area of knowledge? The answer is a mixed answer.

It is similarly mixed with reference to other linkages: to the sexual linkage, for example. In our business civilization there is less overt tyranny of one sex over another than has been the rule in human history—which means that a double influence toward psychological maturity is exerted: men are less able than they once were to satisfy their need for significance through childish forms of domination; and women are more able to develop their full individual powers, so that they are less driven to try to win security and significance through childish forms of submission. All this promises the gradual development of a type of enriched companionship between men and women in which the maturity of each will be encouraged. On the other hand, our business civilization has made sex—like everything else—into a commodity to be made attractive to as wide a consumer public as possible. This has meant that a woefully immature brand of sex has been put on the market by everyone from motion picture producers to makers of underwear, from perfume advertisers to writers of "slick" romances. Also, it must be observed, an economics that is devoted to earning money rather than to the ordering of a household almost inevitably makes human relations—even those of husband and wife—secondary to considerations of profit and prestige. Has our economy, then, fostered sexual maturity or immaturity? The answer is mixed.

It is no less mixed where our linkages of empathy and philosophy are concerned. Industrialization has made alike

for the unifying of all mankind in bonds of mutual related-
ness—so that it has bred the concept of "one world"—and
for the dividing of mankind into nations, classes, and "advanced" and "backward" peoples: these latter fit objects for
imperialistic exploitation. Also, because it has largely taken
from the ordinary person his pre-industrial sense of *belonging*
to his society—of being securely and significantly part of it—
our economic system has gradually driven that ordinary person to seek membership in some exclusive-interest group that
is set over against other groups. He joins a trade association,
or a manufacturers' association, or a union, or a group dedicated to the perpetuation of racial superiority; and in each
instance, he gains a sense of belonging by making it less likely
than before that his generous imagination will extend to include those human beings that are outside the select group.

The total effects of industrial capitalism upon human maturing are, in brief, not easy to measure. We have public
opinion polls. We do not yet have public maturity polls. For
maturity lies deep. It is not something that can be determined
by the asking of a few "opinion" questions that skitter lightly
across the surface of the mind. Since our economic system
has become so dominant a force that no aspect of our life—
domestic, religious, educational, recreational—is beyond its
reach or exempt from its influence; and since psychological
maturity is man's next imperative, we must set ourselves
seriously to the task of trying to measure, on the maturity
scale, the character structure that our business civilization
has encouraged into being.

III

In his speech on "Measures to Resist Philip," Demosthenes is reported to have said: "It is impossible, I say, to have a high and noble spirit while you are engaged in petty and mean employment; whatever be the pursuits of men, their character must be similar." This is sound psychology—and it suggests the type of measure that must be applied to our economic order.

The "pursuits of men" exert a strong and various influence upon the character structures of men. They establish habits of selective awareness; determine what men will see in a given situation, and what they will pass over without seeing. They cause men to value certain aspects of their own natures and to minimize the importance of others. They bring about the repetition of certain activities and experiences until these are converted into habits and attitudes. They direct the ambitions of men, and determine whom they will classify as friend and whom as enemy. Thus Demosthenes was not engaging in oratorical flamboyance when he said that it was impossible "to have a high and noble spirit" while "engaged in petty and mean employment." He was talking hard sense about the manner in which the nature that is born in each individual is shaped into character. A later man of insight was talking about the same thing when he declared the impossibility of serving God and Mammon—"For where your treasure is, there will your heart be also." There will your mind be; and your allegiance; and your will. Where the pursuits of men make for *part*-seeing, men do not achieve *whole*-seeing; where they make for ego-centered seeing, men do not achieve empathic seeing. If there are any laws of the psychological universe, certainly this is one of them.

Whenever our economic order is challenged, its supporters point with pride to the fact, already noted, that it has raised the material standard of living in those countries where it has been the dominant order. The constant reiteration of this fact would seem to imply that, under industrial capitalism, the raising of the human standard of living has been chief among the "pursuits of men"—that *this* has been the main focus of their attention and energy; that *this* has determined their definitions of success and failure. If such were the case, capitalism could clearly show itself to be a force for man's psychological maturing: it would constantly invite him to take on creative responsibility, to employ his imagination to understand the needs of other people, to see the human being as whole and as member of a whole humanity. The plain fact, however, is otherwise: the raising of the standard of living has been, not a chief pursuit, but a by-product; the chief pursuit has been money-making. Where a conflict has arisen between money-making and raising the standard of living, it has been the former that has taken precedence.

The proofs of this are manifold. A glaring proof, for example, is to be found in the current housing situation. If the dominant aim of real-estate associations and the building trades was to provide the best available housing for the greatest possible number of families in the shortest possible period of time—in order that men, women, and children might be able to enjoy a sound material basis for their family life—

would those associations and trades be maintaining an expensive lobby in Washington to fight all programs for low-cost housing? An equally glaring proof is to be found in the policies of organized medical groups: policies that show far less interest in extending medical services to all who need them than in protecting a vested professional monopoly. What is true in these instances is equally true in others. A person would, for example, have to be naïve almost beyond belief to maintain that motion picture producers, cattle men, members of the boards of directors of steel corporations and coal mines, public relations experts, textile manufacturers, members of the Dairy Men's League, and all the rest, have as their chief pursuit the raising of the human standard of living, with the making of money a happy by-product. People who have goods and services to sell need customers. So long as those customers can buy, therefore, there will seem to be an almost inevitable correlation between a system geared to high production and a standard of living that is on the up-and-up. But the slogan "What is good for business is good for you" is so clearly a half-truth at best that it might well be modified to read, "What is good for business may also, fortuitously, be good for you."

Other proofs of the fact that money-making has been the chief pursuit fostered by industrial capitalism are almost painfully easy to assemble. We might point, for example, to the long exploitation of women and children in mills and factories—and the long fight put up, by the owners, against any legislation to protect these workers. We might point to the practices of imperialism. Now that the glamor of "Christian imperialism" has worn off, we begin to take stock of certain facts that should be far from flattering to our Western ego. We learn that the imperialists who took over the destinies of "backward" countries destroyed, in large measure, the native crafts of those countries and yet refused to encourage their industrialization—thus ruthlessly lowering the standard of living under the pretext of bringing to the benighted the blessings of Western civilization.

Another fact, also, about our strange economy is that it has never been interested in the whole human being, but only in those aspects of his nature from which some monetary profit could be derived. An individual might be important to the system as a worker—a person who could be hired to make certain motions of his hands that would contribute to the production of salable goods. He might be important as a consumer—a person who could be persuaded to turn over his money in exchange for goods. He might be important as an investor—a person with surplus money that could be "hired" to work for a corporation. He might be important as an inventor of new things to be sold. He might be important as the possessor of such psychological know-how as could be relied upon to turn hesitant consumers into eager ones. He might be important as a possessor of prides, ambitions, and affections *to the extent that these could be converted into a program of spending.* He might be important as a possessor of a "distinguished name" if this name could be hired as advertising copy. But man *as man* has held slight interest for our economy. For him to grow into full maturity might mean that he would have rich inner resources with which to entertain himself; and that he would be unsusceptible to those competitive prestige appeals that are the delight of advertisers; and that he would feel a deep insistent concern about the rights of the dispossessed. For him to grow into such full maturity would, therefore, make him far less valuable as a source of profit-making than he is in his adult immaturity.

There are two other major counts on which our economy must be rated as something less than a maker of maturity. One of these—which we have already appraised elsewhere— is that it discourages man from using to the limit his human capacity for foresight and over-all planning. Not only does it discourage this on the level of the total economy—where it is made to seem unpatriotic not to leave the common welfare at the mercy of many separate competitive interests— but also on the level of individual and family life. Through its advertising, it has persistently tried to make immediate temptation so irresistible that the individual will spend what he has—even though this may mean the diversion of his funds from more important ends. Through its structure of credit buying and installment buying, it has persistently encouraged families to accept the illusion that large payments are small —thus persuading them to mortgage their futures. The image of man as a "good consumer" is, in brief, often more compatible with that of man as a perpetual impulsive child than with that of him as a mature being of foresight and responsibility.

The other count against our economy is that it has, all too often, fostered mental dishonesty. The term "free enterprise" for example, has been tenaciously used, because of its popular appeal, even by those—or perhaps chiefly by those—who have long since put behind them the practices of free enterprise and who are intent to control the market through monopolies and cartels. The term "government interference" has been recognized as one that would make the plain American bristle with belligerence—and has been used accordingly. But the very corporation that uses it may be making vast profits out of "government interference" in the form of protective tariffs. When, as a matter of fact, the "free enterprise" system breaks down—as during the depression—the government is supposed to rescue it from its predicament. But it is not supposed to ask embarrassing questions about the *why* of the breakdown; and it *is* supposed, as quickly as possible, to join in the general pretense that all is well and that the breakdown was, in fact, only a minor adjustment in a system "fundamentally sound." We might point to another curious dishonesty: the fact that stockholders are encouraged to think of themselves as active partners in the corporations that "hire" their money —so that they have not only an income bias, but also a prestige bias, in favor of the policies of those corporations. To dispel this illusion of "partnership," a small stockholder has only to attend one meeting and to try to express one opinion that goes counter to the intentions of the big stockholders.

Because ours is a "business civilization," moreover, various institutions that are presumably non-economic in their aims have been relegated to positions of such dependence upon the economic order that they, too, learn to rationalize, compromise, and practice a multitude of small dishonesties. This is true of religious institutions—many of which have learned so adroitly to pretend that you can serve God and Mammon that they now believe it themselves. It is true, also, of educational institutions—many of which have learned only too well and too painfully that the mental activities of their students must be confined to "safe" areas.

Where mental dishonesty is made to seem like common sense, or like a fine patriotism, the full maturing of men and women is not likely to be the rule.

I V

From a psychiatric point of view, it may be, however, that the chief indictment of our economic system is its employment of fear as a weapon and its breeding of fear as a by-product. Through long pre-psychological ages there may have been good reason for men to believe that fear was the "natural" stimulus to action; for it is, we know, biologically true that the presence of an immediate danger means an increase in physical energy with which to meet the danger—or flee from it. Also, foresight has seemed to involve, by and large, an element of fear: a sense of future hazards. When, therefore, the final break with feudalism was made, it seemed logical enough, to those who gave the new economy its rationale, to make "competition the life of trade" and fear of privation the chief stimulus to effort. In that period of history, moreover, fear was still the one chief tool for maintaining order throughout the total society—a tool justified by a deep-lying distrust of man's nature. The Church relied on fear of Hell to keep people in the straight and narrow path of orthodoxy. Teachers relied on fear of the rod to keep children's eyes on their books. Parents and political rulers relied on fear to prevent the breaking of arbitrary laws. It would have been a major miracle, under the circumstances, for the new economy to have repudiated fear as a stimulus. Its present belief in the efficacy of fear can best, perhaps, be regarded as residual: it tenaciously hangs on even after similar beliefs in other departments of our life have been progressively discarded under the influence of modern researches into our human nature.

Whatever the historic justification may be, the fact remains that the use to which fear is put by the economic order goes counter to much that we now know about ourselves. We know, for example, that children do not learn best when they are frightened: that the same bodily process that releases energy for the meeting of danger inhibits the higher processes of the mind—those processes that might otherwise cause indecision and deliberation and prevent readiness of action. This is a nice balance provided by nature; but it emphatically discourages the use of fear as a stimulus to learning or to any other activity that involves the mind. We know also, now, that long-sustained fear produces apathy rather than energy: that the constantly anxious person is an ill person, not one full of zest and push. We know that fear and hostility are co-partners in evil: where there is habitual fear, there is an impulse to strike out at someone cast in the role of enemy. We know that the victim of such hostility may not be the person responsible for the fear: he may be anyone available— a child in the home, a wife, a fellow worker, the member of some minority group; he may, in a sense, be *everyone* with whom the frightened person comes into contact. We know that fear makes for concentration on the self—not on the objective work that one is doing—and that it thus acts to prevent emotional maturing.

Few, today, would argue that our economic system gives most people a fine sense of confidence—in themselves and in the dependability of the culture. Everywhere men, women, and children are afraid. Tests, for example, relative to the fears of children in the ten-year-old group show that a dominant fear is that of the father's losing his job. This means that we are distorting our children with a fear that is laid upon them at a time of life when they are helpless to do anything about it. Not only the children of men, but the men themselves, are everywhere afraid of losing their jobs—or of not getting an advance—or of being laid on the shelf in middle life. They and their wives are afraid of not making a good impression, of not being liked by the right people, of not being invited to the right places.

Ours has become a fear-economy—and to that extent, it is an economy inimical to the full maturing of the human individual.

V

At a recent Harvard Commencement, the president of the University made a significant salutation to those who were receiving their degrees in the School of Business. They were now equipped, he told them, to enter "the oldest of the arts and the youngest of the professions."

This was not merely a piece of clever phrasing. He spoke a

truth at once grim and hopeful. Business, thus far, has been an art, not a profession. It has been an art that anyone could practice—without recognized standards; without social obligations and responsibilities; with only a keen sense of how to make profits. As long as things have been made to move from producer to seller to buyer, business has been "good." Whether or not the goods have been good has been a minor consideration. Whether or not they have been good for those who bought them—for their complete development as human beings—has been an even more minor consideration.

If the president of Harvard spoke truth, however, a change is under way: business is beginning to be a profession. This would mean that more and more of the men and women engaged in business would be giving some thought to the social effects of what they do; would be exhibiting a social awareness—not merely a profit-awareness—of consequences. The old rationalization, "I'm not in business for my health," would have to be relegated to the scrap heap of human follies before the professional spirit could really claim the economic sphere as its own. For the businessman who was a professional man would be in business not only for his own health, but for that of his fellows—not only for their physical health, but for their psychological health as well.

The fact is that our society, as we saw in the preceding chapter, is a product of competing philosophies. Sooner or later, unless our nation is to face a swift decline, we will have to choose among them—and build our individual habits and our institutions in terms of the choice we make. R. M. MacIver has pointed straight at our problem when he has written,

We are a democracy, but . . . we are offending against it all the time. The central conception of democracy, that which gives it its vitality underneath, is the conception that it is the person as person that counts; the person not as property owner, not as the member of any class, not as the child of wealth or prestige, not as belonging to this or that race or group or religion, but the person as person; the conception that as a person he should be given equal rights and equal opportunities with others . . .[1]

To the extent that we accept this philosophy as ours, we accept the philosophy of man's maturing—and we are obligated to repudiate any system, however profitable in terms of dollars and cents, that finds it an advantage to keep man immature. When the chief pursuit of men is that of creating conditions favorable to human maturity, our economic order will itself have to outgrow its present childish standards and take on stature commensurate with its responsibility.

[1] "The Need for a Change of Attitude," in *Civilization and Group Relationships*, p. 4. New York, Harper and Brothers, 1945.

EIGHT

THE PLAY OF POLITICS
ON THE MIND

THE NEWS today is that politics is a thing of the mind—of everybody's mind. Not only the psychological and social scientists, but the physical scientists as well, have awakened to the fact that what happens to us *politically* will in large measure determine what happens to us in every other sense; and what happens to us politically, now and in the future, will depend upon our mental and emotional make-up.

The problem of how to organize a society is still among the most difficult of all the problems we have to solve. Perhaps it is the most difficult—since even man's original stark problem of wresting food and shelter from the natural universe has become, now, more political than physical. It is the most difficult because it involves the basic relationship of the individual—his rights and properties—to the social group; and it involves, also, the relationships among organized groups—nations—that are variously strange to one another, variously in competition, variously a prey to their memories of the past, and variously mature and immature in the attitudes they bring to the settling of disagreements and in the methods they employ.

Rightly, politics is *politeia:* an activity having to do with the rational organization of social goods. Prevalently, it is an activity in which we are tacitly licensed to work off our personal and group hostilities and to get what we can for ourselves. Calling for the utmost maturity of motives and methods, and the keenest possible awareness of long-range cause and effect, politics has, by common practice, become a "game" in which men are expected to behave like grown-up children. In no other major area of life has immaturity enjoyed such good standing.

A certain character in one of Edwin Arlington Robinson's poems is sizing up a personal and political crisis, and, in particular, one individual upon whom the destinies of many depend. In a kind of despair, he says,

> ". . . we are at the mercy of a man
> Who if the stars went out would only laugh."[1]

In these times, when not only our personal and national fate, but the whole fate of mankind is at stake, it often seems that we are at the mercy of men who, if the stars should fall, would continue to play out the old game of politics with the old

[1] From "Lancelot" in *Collected Poems*, p. 372. Copyright, 1920, by Thomas Seltzer. Used by permission of The Macmillan Company, publishers.

flippancy, according to the old cynical rules, and with the unregenerate ego in command. Among these men, moreover, we must in honesty number ourselves: we are at the mercy of our own political immaturity. We may not be among those who go in for "horse trading" in smoke-filled rooms; or who pour out platform promises that no one expects to be kept; or who specialize in belligerent gestures toward some other nation. But unless we are rare exceptions to the rule, we are among those who enable our domestic and foreign policies to remain immature by "the consent of the governed."

Our American republic can best be described, perhaps, as the formulation of an hypothesis: namely, that average human beings can become capable of self-government. This is, in all likelihood, the most complimentary hypothesis regarding the nature of man that has ever been given political expression. If we are to deserve the compliment and the chance it offers us to grow up into political competence, we must try to estimate what our political attitudes are and how those attitudes have come about.

II

One glaring fact strikes us in the face: namely, that political practices are, for the most part, hostile practices. The second glaring fact is that we take such hostility for granted. Whether at the local level or the international, we are surprised when we find a disinterested concern for the "rational organization of social goods" but not at all surprised to find man maneuvering against man, party against party, nation against nation. Everywhere in politics the accepted image is the "fight-and-grab image." This is tantamount to saying that the accepted image is that of people who are licensed to act out their impulsive, irresponsible, ego-centered immaturity.

Our most immediate danger lies at the international level; for it is here that the "fight-and-grab image" is most likely to be translated into total disaster. G. B. Chisholm has said, "We need to remind ourselves repeatedly that man has done his best to kill large numbers of other men." [2] Thus flatly stated, without pomp or circumstance, or reference to "national honor," our historic preoccupation with killing seems a sinister comment upon what we are: what we are by nature, or conditioning, or both.

Why has man "done his best to kill large numbers of other men"? Why has he not been able—again in Chisholm's words —to live "permanently in a state of peace with his fellow men"? This is a psychological question. Also, however, it is a *psychosocial* question: it has to do with the social influences that have played upon our natures.

The older view of man—the limited psychological view— was that he was essentially pugnacious: a born killer who will live even in temporary peace only if social restraints keep him in line. The newer, psychosocial view is that while man may be a "natural" killer when his life is directly threatened, he becames a *warrior* only if social conditioning has made him so. Modern man is rarely put into a position where he kills for "natural" reasons: where he responds to an immediate danger with immediate self-defensive action. In most

[2] From *The Future of Psychiatry and the Human Race*. Address before the Annual Meeting of the American Psychiatric Association, 1947.

of his enterprises of killing he acts for social and political reasons.

There is hope in the psychosocial view; none in the old limited psychological view. As we come to understand the full strength of social conditioning, we begin to realize that we accept the policy of "killing large numbers of men" because custom and tradition have made that policy acceptable to us. It is not beyond reason, therefore, with our knowledge of "conditioned responses," to think that our attitudes can be altered. The practical question is whether they can be altered fast enough, in enough minds, to insure human survival. Dead men not only tell no tales; also, they build no civilization. Of all our pressing political problems, then, the most pressing is that of preventing a war that will prevent our having a human future. Can we outgrow the "fight-and-grab image" and come to the point where we are ready to cherish a more mature image of political man?

III

If we are thus to grow, we must understand both our own "hostility potential" and the manner in which we are now encouraged to turn this into overt word and action.

A mature man may set himself strongly against specific persons and policies. He may marshal all his energies and resources to oppose them. But he does so in behalf of some positive value that he attaches to human life and human experience. Only the immature man takes a pervasively hostile attitude toward his world: wears a chip on his shoulder; expects other people to gyp him; classifies every foreigner as a "dirty foreigner"; has an elephant's memory for past slights; enjoys other people's defeats; derives most of his sense of significance from belonging to some "in group" that he can feel to be in sharp contrast to some "out group"; likes to stir other people up to mutual animosities; is prone to exaggerated angers in response to small stimuli—so that the stranger who accidentally jogs his elbow on the streetcar, for example, becomes a "fool" and a "nitwit"; makes a moral virtue of unswerving partisanship; chooses the groups he joins in terms of their exclusiveness rather than of his liking for other members; has daydreams in which he is always getting the upper hand of somebody else, or telling somebody off; feels "alive" only when actually or vicariously involved in conflict.

That such a man is a trouble-maker in a home or a community we recognize readily enough. Wherever he wields his influence there are likely to be tensions, irrational angers, quarrels that stem from insufficient causes, hurt prides, misunderstandings, bitter competitiveness, ruthlessly damaged reputations, and a general irritable readiness for a fight. What we have scarcely begun to realize is that this trouble-maker acts, in all the areas of his life, much as we are all permitted—or even encouraged—to act in the political area. As though we had set this area aside as a place for letting off steam and venting our otherwise pent-up hostilities, we put the basic ordering of our life at the mercy of our less mature emotions.

One common element in our "hostility potential" is *ethnocentrism:* an emotional tie-up with our own group, so that we accept all its attitudes and practices as more right and reasonable than those of other groups. Psychologically, there is nothing mysterious about ethnocentrism. Every child goes through a long period of dependence when it has to make such emotional security as it can out of belonging, by heart and habit, to that tiny portion of the world that comprises "its" world. Its experience of being approved is inseparably tied up with doing what is approved, not by people on the other side of the world, but by its own family unit. Its sense of competence is inseparably tied up with learning the rules and skills useful in its immediate environment. Its power to make its feelings understood—and therefore to get what it wants—is tied up with its power to speak a certain language. Thus, strong emotional ties with the group are established long before the child is old enough to make comparisons and independent judgments. If he is surrounded by adults who encourage him to get the feel of the larger world and to understand that the part is only a part, his native ethnocentrism will not halt his psychological maturing. He will learn that affection for the familiar, and practical responsibility toward it, are compatible with good will toward other groups and a rational exercise of his discriminatory powers. But few people, in any culture, are thus conditioned toward maturity. Most of them grow up in an environment where they are more likely to win approval by unquestioning loyalty than by affection tempered with discrimination. Such independence as most people assert, therefore, is itself immature in quality: an ego-centered adolescent rebellion briefly directed against adult mores without being directed toward anything in particular. Or "independence" may take the form of an intellectual relativism that is likewise immature: a repudiation of ethnocentrism in favor of an abdicating conviction that one thing is as good as another and that there are no standards by which to judge one culture as better than another.

Most people, in brief, come to their adulthood emotionally prepared to think their own group right on all counts, and to think of other groups as "wrong," "dangerous," or "backward" precisely to the degree that they differ from the familiar or set themselves up in opposition to it.

Certain of our institutions make tepid efforts to build more inclusive habits of thinking and feeling: thus, most churches, schools, and universities gingerly suggest the oneness of mankind and the multiple backgrounds from which our culture has derived. But in time of crisis, the vast majority of them swing back into undiluted ethnocentricity; and even when there is no crisis, few of them go at the building of the supra-ethnic mind with any great vigor.

Our political institutions not only fail to build the supra-ethnic mind, but shout "treason" at those who try to build it with more than an absent-minded, half-hearted zeal. From the precinct machine to the halls of Congress, political practices encourage people to be "loyal," to be blindly partisan, to be ready for verbal or actional hostility against an opposing group. Thus ethnocentrism, as one chief factor in our "hostility potential," is so rewarded that it is likely to flourish in undiminished vigor—and untransformed immaturity—through all the years of most people's lives.

Closely related to it is a second element in our "hostility potential": *xenophobia*—fear of the stranger, and therefore a readiness to hate that stranger. The roots of *xenophobia*, like those of *ethnocentricity*, must be looked for in childhood: in the fact that security and familiarity there seem to be the same thing. But in its adult expressions, *xenophobia*—again, like *ethnocentricity*—is a sign of arrested development. It means that the grown-up person, who supposedly has powers of discrimination, makes an automatic negative response that has nothing to do with known characteristics of the stranger but only with the fact of his strangeness. Human beings are perfectly capable of outgrowing *xenophobia*. But most of them, in melancholy fact, grow into it rather than out of it: as adults they have more automatic prejudices against more groups of outsiders than the child has. What is a mere shyness in the child becomes, all too often, active hostility in the socially conditioned adult; and one reason why it becomes so is that political practices make it so. In political circles, on the local or the international level, it is rarely considered a sufficient loyalty to be neutral toward the "outsider" until all the facts are in; only a readiness for hostility is considered enough to make a person rate as a "good" party member or patriot.

A third element in our "hostility potential" must be noted. We are born with the will to survive. This expresses itself, when necessary, in self-defensive action. The emotional accompaniment of such action is hostility to that which threatens us. It takes an emotional reaction of this sort, not merely a detached awareness of danger, to "charge" our body with extra energy. It is not the *fact* of danger, but the *feeling* of danger, that sets adrenalin going in the blood stream. This animal equipment that we have for self-defense is one that can be so culturally conditioned that we will develop the proper hostility feeling, and will take overt action, not only against a known enemy in our actual presence, but against whole groups and nations that we have been told to accept as enemies. Part of the age-old art of the politician is precisely that of getting people to feel that the hostile action they take against another group is action dictated by their own need for self-defense.

There is a fourth element in our "hostility potential": namely, the angers, frustrations, fears, boredoms, and disappointments that mark our individual experience, and that leave, as it were, a sedimentary deposit in our unconscious that can easily be stirred up to muddy the psychological waters. Virtually everyone has stored up enough latent hostility to make him ready for aggressive action when he finds that he can win approval and reward by such action. The daily pattern of modern "civilized" life discourages the individual from converting most of his fears and angers into direct and immediate action. It discourages him, also, from striking out at the actual object of his emotion—which is as likely as not to be his "boss" or someone equally equipped for destructive retaliation. His angers, therefore, become pent-up, cumulative irritations and hostilities; and they become "displaced"—that is, directed not against their original object, but against a "surrogate" object. This "surrogate" may, at the simplest level, be a chair that is handy to be kicked; at a more complex level, however, it may become the opposing political party, some racial minority, or some nation on the other side of the world. The latter type of "enemy" offers great "advantages" over the former: for while a man looks silly kicking a chair, he can—our political assumptions being what they are—look brave, loyal, and patriotic kicking an enemy who has been officially labeled as "kickable." He may even be appointed to office or receive a regular monthly stipend from his government if he kicks hard enough and according to prescribed rules.

What we have been saying here is that we humans are made of psychological stuff and psychological experiences that make us potential haters; potential killers. We are not fated by our nature, however, to convert this destructive potential into action. Whether or not we do so is largely determined by our culture, by the institutions that shape us.

To the extent that a culture wants its citizens to become mature men and women it will encourage them to outgrow their ethnocentrisms and xenophobias—translating these into specific affections that are compatible with general good will. It will also encourage them to think of self-defense in terms of the "rational organization of social goods," not in terms of periodic violence. Finally, it will aim to set up institutions —domestic, educational, and economic—that will lessen the likelihood that unliquidated hostilities will become stored up in the individual. Knowing, however, that such hostilities do accumulate, it will not try to build guilt feelings around them in certain areas of life while rewarding their violent and "displaced" release in some specified area—certainly not in such a vital area as the political. Rather, it will try to give people a maximum chance to mitigate their hostilities through a sense of competence and through constructive and co-operative action.

One of the saddest indictments that can be brought against most of the political practices of men—including those in our own culture—is that they reward hostility and penalize inclusive good will. Thus, they infect society at its roots with the virus of adult immaturity: of power exercised in excess of understanding.

IV

It would be unfair in the extreme to leave the impression that *all* our political attitudes and behaviors have been immature, that in this area there has been no place for maturity to exercise itself. The obvious case is otherwise.

When Benjamin Franklin called us a nation of politicians, he might have meant either of two things: that the average American will get into a partisan political argument at the drop of a hat; or that the average American brings to the problem of political organization a certain zest, mental resilience, and ingenuity that could have no political expression except in a culture based on "consent of the governed."

Traditionally, the American has *enjoyed* politics. He has enjoyed politics immaturely—playing it irresponsibly as a game, or working off his angers and hostilities through it, or finding in the experience of blind partisanship an easy satisfaction of his need to belong. Also, however, he has enjoyed politics maturely: trying to match laws to ideals, tinkering the social mechanism back into running order when it has broken down, making one social invention after another, dedicating himself to causes larger than those of his own self-interest, bridging partisan gaps and working for the common good. Just as his immaturity is seen in his smoking-car arguments, his allegiance to the straight ticket, his tolerance of intolerable "machines," his periodic orgies of witch-hunting, his patriotic braggadocio, his self-centered lobbying, and his sallies into imperialism, his political maturity is expressed in the extension of the right to vote to more and more elements of the population, in laws to protect the helpless and to increase opportunities for growth, in a general gearing of his mind to evolutionary rather than revolutionary methods of change, and even, we might say, in his willingness to repent of his gross immaturities and to try to undo the harm they have done.

In our own time, because of the world crisis, immaturity at work in the political area can do irremediable harm. If it acts itself out in terms of its own perverse and limited logic, maturity may not long have any chance to operate. Meanwhile, however, there are developments to be noted that both express a growing political maturity and encourage its further growth.

The first of these, still largely unnoticed, is a development that is working to lessen hostile partisanship. I refer to the activities of those bodies of men and women—commissions or committees—specially appointed to explore some social problem and to report findings to the constituted authorities and to the public. In recent years, for example, mayors' commissions on race relations have served to high-light racial problems in urban areas and to bring the combined wisdom of men and women from many walks of life so to bear that these problems will be handled in terms of facts rather than partisan fancies. Governors' commissions on fair employment practices have served similar ends; so have housing commissions, commissions on public health, commissions on juvenile delinquency, commissions on city and regional planning; so, notably, has the President's Commission on Civil Rights.

All such commissions deal with matters that are "political." Not only do they have to do with "the rational organization of social goods" but also they involve government, officers of government, and that public whose opinion either supports or defeats government. Psychologically, however, what distinguishes these bodies is that they substitute the "exploration" pattern for the "hostility" pattern, and non-partisanship for partisanship. Most of the men and women who sit on these commissions are members of one or another political party. They may even be "die-hard" Republicans or Democrats. But *as commission members,* they are asked to put their fixed loyalties aside long enough to look at objective facts. They are asked to be producers of social insight for the common good. Both the approval-pattern and the responsibility-pattern within which they are thus asked to operate are of a new order in the political area: they invite the individuals involved to grow up themselves even while they are gathering facts on which our society can grow up.

A second factor making for political maturity has attracted even less notice—because it is less obviously a political factor. I refer, here, to the movement of parent education. Such education, carried on through agencies as various as churches, state universities, child study associations, and the National Congress of Parents and Teachers, is bringing more and more reliable psychological information to the mothers and fathers of America. Part of this information has to do simply with how to feed a baby or what to do till the doctor comes. But far more of it has to do with the factors in the home, school, and community that make for the mental, emotional, and social growth of the child. Here, there, and everywhere the word is being spread that adult behaviors that encourage fears and hostilities in children are lessening those children's chances of a happy and fruitful adulthood. Quite specifically the word is being spread, with sound psychological references to back it up, that a home is not a good home, no matter how many "advantages" it offers, if it is bringing up children to distrust the human race, to label various groups as "inferior," to think of violent action as the "natural" way to resolve differences, to identify "loyalty" with acute ethnocentrism and xenophobia. Quite specifically, also, the word is being spread that democracy begins at home: within the four walls of home where children are given a chance to speak out their wants and perplexities instead of suppressing them for fear of ridicule or punishment; where children are given a chance to learn social competence and responsibility by being in on the family problems and plans. As parent education becomes more and more general, we will have in our adult population more and more people who have savored and enjoyed a type of human drama that is not that of blind partisanship.

A third factor that is encouraging us to political maturity is the world crisis. This has reached a point where more and more people realize that it is too serious to be treated as a game. Increasingly, therefore, they are ready to bring to it the type of honest thought that they bring to the experience of problem-solving in other areas. Even the old immature pleasure of overcoming an enemy is beginning to seem too costly to be indulged. Human survival begins to seem more important.

A fourth factor that is helping Americans to outgrow their political immaturity is the type of voluntary association in which people are asked to think about "the rational organization of social goods" and then to work by non-partisan political means for the achievement of legislation consonant with these goods. Such organizations, for example, as the League of Women Voters, the Union for Democratic Action, and the National Congress of Parents and Teachers make it their business to help their members come to some mature understanding of both political issues and political methods. The last named of these organizations may not, in the common mind, be rated as "political." But anyone who has studied its legislative program relative to education, health, and world understanding or who has checked up on its influence upon state legislatures must see that it is political in a double sense: it works for specific bills and against others; and it educates its own people to think of political activities in terms of "social goods."

The pro-social voluntary association in America is our great unsung laboratory for the making of citizens. It is the means—in many cases, the only means—whereby the average citizen is encouraged to feel other than helpless about the affairs of his society. Whether the association be local, national, or international; and whether it works to promote child welfare, community recreation, aid to the needy, public health, adult education, inter-faith understanding, international understanding, or racial justice, it is made up of people of different party affiliations, different creeds, different nationalities, often different races and different economic classes. In such an association, a readiness for mutual understanding is encouraged and rewarded with approval; a carrying over of fixed partisanships and prejudices is discouraged. In it, therefore, men and women of good will have the blessed chance to care about something that relates to the common welfare; to do so in the company of people who have been permitted to take off their artificial labels of party and class; and to achieve actual results that both change society, in some measure, and build their citizen-confidence that they can bring about further change when it is needed.

Yet another factor is making for maturity: the old image of the "police state" or the "umpire state"—which presupposed conflict—is being gradually replaced by the image of the "service state." This latter image does not make conflict between individuals or groups the major social expectation. Instead, it sees organized society as a means for satisfying basic human needs and providing basic opportunities. The transformation of the "police state" into the "service state" has actually, in America, been going on for a long time. This change, however, has been largely concealed by the fact that the issues of social welfare have had to be worked out, fought out, and argued out along the old lines of party antagonisms and vested interests. In the game of politics, social legislation has often been reduced to the status of a football. Nonetheless, the trend away from the fight-and-grab image toward the service image has been too strong to be checked even by political bosses or the filibuster. As Americans progressively learn to think in terms of social goods, they take on political maturity.

As an added factor—or perhaps as an expression of all the factors already named—we must point to the fact that even party "loyalties" are not what they once were. Machine politicians are becoming more and more painfully aware of the fact that they cannot win elections unless they win the support of the political "independents"—the men and women who vote according to their own appraisal of candidates and issues; not according to the party line. This fact not only testifies to a movement away from the older, automatic hostilities, but it hastens that movement by requiring that even professional politicians think occasionally about issues and qualifications.

It may be that mature political habits are being formed among us more rapidly than we notice—our attention being fixed, for the most part, on the drama of conflict. In any event, the news today is that politics is a thing of the mind. It will be good news indeed when maturity of mind makes politics the sort of activity it ought to be: a rational effort to organize the goods of life for the good of life.

NINE

WHAT WE READ, SEE, AND HEAR

FOUR INFLUENCES continually at work in the shaping of our character are newspapers, radio, movies, and advertising. We need, now, to ask the psychosocial question whether the influence of these has, in the main, been for or against our maturing.

Every day—sometimes "every hour on the hour," sometimes all morning, or all afternoon, or all day long; almost always at breakfast and on the journey home at night— these influences come into the lives of millions of people. Walt Whitman once wrote about a child that went forth each day and became what he saw. A later Whitman, writing about what comes into the lives of people each day through newspapers, radio, movies, and advertising, might well ask whether that which comes into their lives they themselves become. Surely, all this daylong and lifelong bombardment by news, entertainment, and announcements of things to be bought must have some effect. As a matter of fact, it is more than likely that we might properly be called newspaper-made, radio-made, movie-made, and advertisement-made people. To the extent that this is true, what kind of people, then, are we?

The functions of news-bringing, storytelling, music-making, and goods-selling are obviously basic to our needs. We live by them. In one form or another, man has always lived by them. The human being wants to know what is going on: hence our universal welcome to the news-bringer. We all need, now and then, to be stirred by tales that take us outside ourselves and help us to do the uniquely human thing of entering, through imagination, into the lives of others. In fact, it seems probable that our growth into empathy—so essential to our psychological maturing—depends in no small degree upon our having a chance to live vicariously the lives of many different sorts of people. We need, again, to hear the rhythms of music. We need, for the planning of our practical lives, to know what things are available for our convenience, comfort, and increased efficiency. To this extent it must be said that all these things are good—newspapers, radio, movies, advertising.

Yet it might be more accurate to say that they are potentially good; for, from the point of our psychological maturing, each of them is today a question mark. Is today's newspaper-reading public made wise and informed by its newspaper reading? Is the public that listens to the radio and goes to the movies thereby prepared to make more mature responses to human situations? Is a public that is constantly being importuned to buy things encouraged toward discrimination and self-discipline? It is altogether probable that, in spite of their high technical achievements, their constant accessibility, and their relationship to deep human wants and needs, newspapers, radio, movies, and advertising are doing as much to arrest as to promote our maturing. In many lives, in fact, they appear to weight the scales heavily toward arrested development.

All of these influences are part of a culture marked by vast technical expertness. But all of them, also, it must be remembered, are part of a money-making culture: an economy in which the prime value that attaches to most things produced is their exchange value—their salability. This is no less true of a newspaper or a motion picture than it is of a washing machine. Fundamental in the motivation of each of these character-shaping factors we have named, then, is the producer's need to make profits. The yardstick that the producer applies to what he offers is, first, a financial yardstick; it is not the yardstick of human welfare or human growth into maturity, except as such growth happens to be profitable. Here, therefore, is our peculiar modern situation: every day our minds and characters are receiving the impress of objects and experiences that have been put on the market because they represent the seller's best guess as to what we are ready to buy.

Here, again, we must note the difference between a business and a profession. In a profession, welfare comes first; money-making second. The distinction is a delicate one and hard to make with precision. Nevertheless it is a real one that

makes a notable difference in the spirit and aims of an undertaking. Thus, where money-making is the paramount interest,
a constant search will be made to discover what most people
as they are can be relied upon to like most of the time. What
a few discriminating people like is of no great financial significance. What many people might eventually like if they
were helped to develop their powers of discrimination has
equally little financial import. What most people like once
in a while is of less financial import than what they like most
of the time. Hence, the primary hunt conducted by each of
these four licensed mind-makers has been for a formula that
would insure most people's being attracted most of the time.
Once the formula is set, there is more profit to be derived
from people's remaining *as they are* than from their growing
up to some new level of insight and discrimination. The
essential fact to be noted about each of the four businesses at
hand is that each has found its own particular formula, has
geared its productive set-up to that formula, and therefore
has a vested interest in the public's continued responsiveness
to that formula.

II

The newspaper has discovered that most people most of
the time are interested in some form of catastrophe: a plane
crash, a railroad wreck, a murder, a flood, a scandal, a fight
of some sort. It is an old story that the planes that fly safely,
the trains that reach their destination, the individuals who
live together without murdering each other, the rivers that
flow between their banks, and the men and nations that

transact their affairs and resolve their differences without fighting are not news. Not one of these would yank a man out of his own preoccupations as he passed a newsstand. Not one of them would make him prop up his paper at the breakfast table and become absorbed in reading, to the neglect of his family. To capture the breakfaster, some unusual "happening" must be reported. To keep him turning page after page, one column of unusual "happenings" must follow another. In order to induce that same breakfaster to buy a second paper in the afternoon or evening—or, if possible, even a third—headlines must again shrill the unusual and the catastrophic.

News, in short, must be as different as possible from the average daily routine; for otherwise it will not pull the mind of man out of that routine. The mind of man is, of course, capable of escaping routine through an intensification of awareness; through a deepened sense of values; through becoming sensitized to the subsurface drama of life. But this type of escape cannot be reduced to a formula. It has to do with the growth of the individual toward the unique fulfillment of his powers. It is not only useless, therefore, but actually detrimental, so far as mass production of news is concerned. The formula calls for the constant playing up of the only "escape-from-routine" news that has mass appeal: that is, news about some event that is enough out of the ordinary to give people a thrill without requiring of them any unusual sensitivity or subtlety of insight.

Between the accounts of catastrophe, newspapers do carry a good many items that lie outside the formula and that have their own constant appeal because of certain sustained human interests: weather reports, stock-market reports, household suggestions, real-estate news, educational, religious, and scientific news, and other such. But the primary appeal of a newspaper is the news it brings of happenings that bode ill to someone. Most political news is cast as "fight" news. Most foreign news is similarly cast. Most domestic news that makes the headlines is catastrophic news: someone has been killed, robbed, or assaulted; someone has called a strike; someone has been putting over a raw deal; someone has been arrested; some criminal has escaped; someone is denouncing someone. Most newspapers, in brief, have made the money-making discovery that most people most of the time are more interested in life that has "run off the track" than in life that has "stayed on the track."

Newspapers, therefore, have developed what might be called *a vested interest in catastrophe*. If they can spot a fight, they will play up that fight. If they can uncover a tragedy, they will headline that tragedy.

From the point of view of our psychological maturing all this has obvious significance. It means that day by day, year in and year out, all of us—young as well as old—are being moved to accept a one-sided, distorted view of life. We get life in its hostile and catastrophic patterns more often than in its friendly and constructive patterns. Ours is a culture in which newspapers have influenced most people, from their childhood on, to build the expectation that "eventfulness" is mostly conflict and catastrophe.

To take one example, our public opinion in regard to the

world situation is chiefly shaped by what we read in the newspapers. If what we read is consistently and sharply slanted away from the constructive and peace-seeking activities of men and nations to those that are destructive and belligerent, the opinion we form will be not only one-sided and often erroneous, but it will be fraught with terrible danger to our own future and that of mankind. Our own "hostility potential" will be raised. Our attitudes toward peace-seeking activities will be skeptical and pessimistic. We will be wary and quick to suspect someone of trying to put something over on us. Our major emotional readiness will be for belligerent action—or for such belligerent verbalizing as makes peaceful action more difficult to achieve. We will get a more tingling pride out of having our nation "tell off" another nation than we will out of having it effect a mutual agreement with that nation. When we lay our nickels and dimes on the line for our daily dose of vicarious catastrophe and conflict it is almost as though we were paying the newspapers for getting us ready to commit human suicide.

A striking example of the power of the newspaper "formula" occurred at the time of the formation of the United Nations Organization in San Francisco. It will be remembered that the State Department had ventured a remarkable innovation: it had invited the leading non-partisan voluntary associations of the country to send representatives to the Conference to serve as "consultants." These consultants were privileged to sit in on all major sessions; to confer among themselves about moot problems; to meet with various experts and put their questions and suggestions to these experts; to make recommendations to the appropriate bodies; and, last but not least, to send regular reports back to their organizations. Before long, anxious letters began coming to them from members back home. "We don't understand," these letters said in effect. "You keep sending us word that everything is going well and that a world organization will surely be formed; but our newspapers keep telling us that fights and disagreements among the delegates are so constant that there is little hope of success for the Conference. Are you sure you know the score? We don't want to be fed on false hope."

The situation was a typical one. Newspapers, with their vested interest in catastrophe, were playing up every cross word spoken; magnifying every squabble of orators until it seemed a major crisis—a crisis the developments of which would surely have to be followed in tomorrow's paper as well as in today's.

In one vital respect, however, the situation was atypical. Normally, we of the public have no representatives on hand to give a picture different from the one the newspapers give; at San Francisco, we had such representatives—the consultants. As worried letters kept coming in from the home people, these consultants went to the correspondents and asked why they were persistently trying to make the Conference appear to be a failure. Actually, of course, the correspondents—as individuals and as citizens—did not want it to fail. But *as correspondents* they wanted news that would make the old "formula" appeal. Called to account by the consultants—who represented, through their combined or-

ganizations, a significant slice of the reading public—the
newspapers were persuaded to believe that even good news
might be rated as news. A gradual change became evident
in the reporting of the Conference.

That our newspapers have been in many respects a cultural asset goes almost without saying. With their enormous
coverage of news, they have done wonders to release us from
our old parochialisms and to help us move out of our squeezed
local environments into the total world. Also, in many cases,
they have been valiant exposers of evil and valiant fighters
for the human decencies. Yet the fact remains that their
major appeal has been to the psychological immaturities
still resident in grown men and women.

III

Radio came as something new under the sun. As it flashed
upon the human horizon, it promised a new world. Space,
man's ancient enemy, had been overcome. In an instant's
time, our minds could encircle the globe. Man could be neighbor to man the earth around.

The spectacle of an average person sitting in his average
room before a small boxlike instrument, summoning voices
out of the distance, roused the imagination. The Greeks had
said that a city should be no greater in size than the distance
a man's voice could travel. In the twentieth century, suddenly, a man's voice could travel around the world. How
large, then, should the "city of man" now be?

The man sitting in his small room, moreover, with his
small box, could not only encircle the globe. He could sum-

mon at will voices nearer at hand: voices to sing to him; tell
him news when he wanted news; tell him a story when he
wanted a story; preach him a sermon when he wanted a
sermon.

There was no doubt about it: an amazing new force had
entered our human scene. Would it become a new, major
force for our maturing? Or would it so lend itself to our immaturities that these would become more tenacious than
ever?

Such delicate and difficult questions have never yet yielded
us a simple Yes or No answer. Because of the radio, greatness has poured into our homes from many places and at
many times: great symphonic music, the news of world-
transforming events, great poetry, great speeches, great
drama. Not even the poorest, most inaccessible shack or farm
kitchen has been so mean that greatness—via the radio—
has refused to enter and live there. It would be strange if
all this could happen without some increase in maturity
happening also.

Yet greatness has not been the only thing that has entered
our homes—and our consciousness—over the sound waves.
In a sense, it has been the least of what has entered. Where
one notable program has occupied one band of air for a
scant half hour or less, scores of lesser programs have occupied all the other bands of air all day long and all night long.
The talking, the singing, the playing of instruments, the
making of jokes, the asking of quiz questions, the retailing
of news, and from all stations, at virtually all times, the
ubiquitous advertising of goods—these have become a Ni-

agara of sound. In the total mass, the proportion of greatness to the proportion of littleness has not been encouraging.

Radio remains, and increasingly becomes, a technical triumph. But it would not be an exaggeration to say that nine out of ten of the voices that the listener summons when he turns the dial are the voices of mediocrity—and of immaturity: mediocre actors speaking mediocre lines—or actors who deserve better lines trying to inject meaning into the meaningless; mediocre singers singing mediocre songs; mediocre comedians laboring to make old jokes sound new; mediocre commentators sharing the air with their more penetrating and responsible fellows; mediocre quiz masters asking questions and handing out prizes; mediocre advice-givers responding to deep human perplexities with pat mediocre advice. If, from the point of view of man's maturing, the test we must put to radio is that of its *average* influence or its most frequently exerted influence, the answer is not reassuring.

It is almost as easy to gripe about radio programs as about the weather: they have become as much part of our "atmosphere" as wind and sun; and they seem, sometimes, to be as far removed from our influence. Our wish, here, is not to engage in any such griping. In the first place, appearances to the contrary notwithstanding, there is no unreachable "God" of radio "weather" who resides in a heaven beyond our human reach; there are only men, in skyscrapers or in lesser buildings, who engage, day in and day out, in the business of trying to guess what most people want most of the time or what they can, by sufficient suggestion, be made to want.

From the psychological angle, then, the average level of radio programs betrays our immaturity quite as much as it fosters that immaturity. We have to keep this fact in mind as we analyze the influence that is daily being exerted upon our character structure by this new medium of communication. In the second place, radio programs cannot be evaluated as though they were isolated phenomena in our culture. Powerful as radio corporations are, they are only fragments of a system very much larger than themselves; and they would not have become powerful if their aims and methods had been out of line with the practices of that system or offensive to those conditioned by it.

The plain fact is that the owners and program directors of radio stations have been engaged in an enterprise similar to that of newspaper owners and editors: they have been looking for a formula with which to hold the attention of the greatest possible number of people for the greatest possible period of time. They seem to have discovered two things: that most people, most of the time, want to be entertained; and that the entertainment that has the maximum appeal is that which rouses ready emotions and does not tax the mind. With these "discoveries" as directives, the radio formula has gradually evolved.

One program-building assumption has been that people must not be asked to keep their attention focused on any one thing for more than a few minutes at a time. Thus, each day's program becomes a miscellany; and, daylong and nightlong, it invites the mind to engage in a kind of jumping game. No sooner is the attention given to a news report than

it is diverted to a hillbilly singer or a mystery story or a quiz
program or a comedy program replete with guest singers.
This aspect of the radio formula must be of major concern
to all who care about human maturing. One mark of the
psychological growth of the human being, from infancy
through childhood and into adulthood, is the lengthening
of the attention-span. The immature mind hops from one
thing to another; the mature mind seeks to follow through.
Whatever other influences it may exert for our maturing,
radio is on the side of lifelong immaturity in the constant
invitation it offers us to develop hopscotch minds. For five
minutes, say, we are asked to be in a mind and mood suitable
for an honest consideration of a world crisis. Then, for an
even briefer interval, we are asked to feel that it is of supreme
importance for us to buy a certain brand of dehydrated soup
or to have our winter furs stored at a certain place. Abruptly,
then, a humorist begins to wisecrack—and again our mind
and mood are supposed to be at his command. Such flittering
surface interest in one thing after another militates against
our making a genuinely suitable response to anything. How
many people, for example, who hear an appeal for the starv-
ing children of Europe tucked in between a soap opera and
a singer of folk songs, with advertisements for insulation, are
actually invited to feel what mature human beings should
feel about the starvation of children?

It is, of course, impossible to talk about the radio without
talking about radio advertising. Not only does this contribute
mightily to the hopscotch character of the daily program,
but it has exerted its influence upon each item that makes up

that program. Radio listeners do not, by direct methods, put anything into the coffers of radio producers. It is the advertisers who must keep those coffers filled; and they will not do so unless they are convinced that every program item for which they pay is being heard by potential customers in a suitable frame of mind to buy. The housewife who has just had a good cry over a soap opera is more likely to give uninhibited and friendly response to an advertiser than is a person whose mind has been engaged at a high level of discrimination. Similarly, the man who has just had a good laugh at a comedian's jokes has been softened up into friendliness. From the advertiser's point of view, two things are not good business: programs that put the critical powers of man to work and programs that raise any basic issues about the economic structure within which advertising operates. We shall have more to say about advertising in a later section. Suffice it here to say that, in the radio world, it is an all-powerful influence: it makes it necessary that programs be on the air at all hours of the day and night, every day of the year, whether or not material worth hearing can be provided in such quantity; it makes it necessary that most programs be "relaxing" in their influence; and it performs the odd function of taking that old stock figure, the peddler, off the doorstep and into the living room—there to wheedle as he has always wheedled; there to run off his stock phrases as he has always run them off; but there to invade the family privacy as he has never invaded it before.

When an instrumentality is taken over as a money-making device, those who live by it must seek a money-making formula. Radio has found its formula. Whereas the newspaper has found its vested interest in catastrophe, radio has found it in mediocrity.

IV

Are the movies a force for maturing? To ask that question is, almost, to answer it. Hollywood has become a synonym for vacuity serviced by technical experts: highly profitable vacuity, since a staggering proportion of Americans, young and old, week after week, place themselves under its influence.

Great pictures have come out of Hollywood; and briefly they have heartened us. But when they have had their run, the typical Hollywood production has again taken over— and throughout the thousands of movie theaters of the land, the routine of vacuous inanity has been resumed. Today's pictures are infinitely smoother in their production than those of even a few years ago. Also, they are more sophisticated in their characterization: the villain twirls his mustache less obviously; the "scarlet woman" does not, at her first appearance, advertise her intentions by turning Theda Bara eyes upon her victim. The past few years, moreover, have witnessed certain efforts to give movie plots a third dimension—to add to mere eventfulness some slight consideration of human motives of a less than obvious sort. Yet when we attend revivals of earlier movies, and compare them with those that now make a less flickering appearance upon the screen, we are forced to conclude that the psychological difference is a pin-point difference compared with the technical.

Here we confront the same perplexity as in the case of the radio: how did it happen that this great invention has so developed as to express and encourage immaturity rather than maturity. To be sure, it began as a peep-show gadget; but very quickly it revealed its power for greater things. It could tell a story as no story had ever been told before: with horses galloping, guns firing, crowds milling around; or, more quietly, with people walking in the garden, or hiking over a mountain trail. Where drama had hitherto been confined to a small stage, the motion picture could take place on a stage as wide as the world. As a medium, therefore, of enormous range and flexibility, it might have become the greatest influence in human history for the encouragement of empathic imagination. Not confined, as legitimate drama has been confined, to a few theaters in a few cities, it might have invited the most obscure inhabitant of the most remote village to develop an ever maturing insight into the ways of people, and the needs and fears and hopes of people, everywhere. It was technically equipped to perform this role in our culture; but only fortuitously and rarely has it performed it.

Again, we must note an economic cause: movies soon became big business. Single movies ran into millions for their production. *Ben Hur*, for example, cost six million. Salaries were fabulous. In two years of acting in cowboy films, W. S. Hart earned $900,000. Big business meant that there had to be big capital: bankers had to be enlisted. The enlistment of big bankers meant that a formula must be found for making big business grow continually bigger.

Hollywood found its formula. It began to find it in the early days when actors threw custard pies at one another or an escaped convict in prison stripes hid in a basket of clothes on which a housewife had momentarily turned her back. Audiences clapped and shrieked; every frustrated person present got vicarious satisfaction out of seeing the other fellow get it in the face or out of seeing the forces of respectability put to rout.

It began to find its formula when "America's sweetheart" showed her face on the screen. Every man in the audience loved her as he had always hoped he would love some woman; every woman saw in her the type of eternal sweetheart that she herself had hoped to be.

It was finding its formula when it put on male actors who typified "romance." When Valentino stormed the hearts of American women, the story was plain enough for any producer to see: women wanted men who would look into their eyes as their own work-a-day husbands did not look; they wanted men with enough mystery about them to make their least glance glamorous and a little frightening, even; they wanted men in whom kindness and aloofness would be so subtly blended that a relationship with them could never become a routine; but they wanted these men in a daydream situation—not as any actual substitute for the reliable bringer home of the bacon.

It was finding its formula—through a genius who could not be reduced to formula—when a little tramp with a postage-stamp mustache, battered shoes, and a derby hat, took the kicks of the world and walked out of every picture swinging his ridiculous cane in a defeat so jaunty that it amounted to triumph. Charlie Chaplin was Everyman—every man who carries with him his unresolved frustrations, his clumsy good will, and his need to believe that the defeats he suffers are part of fate.

It was finding its formula when the six-shooter hero dashed across the plains on a superb horse that would tolerate no other rider—and rescued the heroine at the last possible moment.

It was finding its formula when, in picture after picture, the erring husband returned to his wife and went down on penitent knees; and when, in picture after picture, the honest small-town hero, with native shrewdness as his only weapon, outsmarted the man from the city; and when the poor girl married a rich husband—and automatically knew just what to do on every occasion that her new setting presented; and when, conversely, the rich girl, deciding that money isn't everything, married her poor lover; and when the erstwhile villain suddenly showed himself as having a heart of gold; and when, in as many ways as ingenuity could devise, the pompous man was made to look like a fool.

What Hollywood discovered—by rule of thumb and box-office returns—was that the sure-fire way to attract people (or at least, most of the people most of the time) is to give them compensatory illusions. Motion pictures became the big business through which unsatisfied men, women, and adolescents in unprecedented numbers were granted a day-dream fulfillment of their hopes. The motion picture did not aim to make these unsatisfied people go forth and take positive action to solve their own problems. It aimed to give them a dream that was in itself so thrilling in comparison with reality that they would return, and return again, for further hours of dreaming. So fixed has this money-making formula become that even novels and dramas of stature and integrity come out of the movie-mill something other than they were: they come out revised to fit the daydreams of the unsatisfied immature.

Fulfillment by fantasy: this is the pattern of psychological immaturity. Fulfillment by a rational, sustained program of action: this is the pattern of psychological maturity. To an overwhelming extent, the Hollywood formula has been on the side of immaturity. Hollywood, we might say, is the enormously profitable enterprise of encouraging millions of people—an estimated 80,000,000 a week in 1940, for example—to find their habitual escape from frustration and boredom in glamorous fantasy. Hollywood, in short, has a vested interest in escapism. Inevitably, therefore, it has a vested interest in emotional immaturity.

V

Advertising is the nation's biggest business. It is also one of the biggest and most continuous psychological influences in our lives. It is literally everywhere. Wherever, by day or night, our eyes and ears are open, we are likely to see or hear some invitation to buy something. It is as though we were surrounded by a vast army of salesmen, each struggling to win our attention; each with something to show us, something for us to buy, something we are made to feel that we *must* buy if we are not to live our lives under a handicap; each trying to get the money we have to spend before someone else gets it.

We do not resent the importunities of these "salesmen." We like to do the sort of wanting that they make us do: the advertisements in a home magazine or a Sunday paper are willingly given a large slice of our attention; and few things yield us more repeated delight than a seed catalogue or the fat catalogue from a mail-order house . . . to say nothing of the windows of clothing stores, hardware stores, book stores, art supply stores, stationery stores. Goods, goods everywhere, and money with which to buy: this is one shape that the American dream has persistently taken; and it has been very far from a bad dream. The ingenuities of men in producing endless things for use, comfort, and convenience have been good ingenuities; and much of the wanting that we do, under the stimulus of advertisements, is good wanting. Much of it ties up soundly with our making of choices and plans. Basic to a high productive economy, in brief, is the process of letting people know what has been produced.

Yet there are psychological questions to ask here: questions that are again tied up with the problem of our individual and cultural maturing. So far as advertisers are concerned—and the producers who employ them—the average man plays only one role that has any significance: that of consumer. His mental and emotional processes are of interest only to the extent that they can be ferreted out and capitalized: used as stimuli to make him buy. Such a one-sided concept of the human being—particularly when almost unlimited resources are used to make it attractive—can scarcely help making for a one-sided development, and therefore a less than fully mature development, of that human being. When he and his fellows, moreover, have in sufficient number and for a sufficient length of time taken such one-sidedness for granted, the whole culture to which they belong will be slanted away from full maturity.

To put the matter succinctly, advertising halts our psychological growth to the extent that it *makes us do too much wanting* and *makes us want things for the wrong reasons.*

It makes us do too much wanting. There is scarcely a waking hour of our lives when we are not told, through some medium, that we ought to pay out money to buy this or that. The cumulative effect of this is fourfold: we are kept always on the edge of material discontent, so that what we have never seems good enough; we are progressively trained to want the ready-made and to think of what we can make ourselves as a poor substitute, so that the pleasures of ownership overshadow the pleasure of creativeness; we are encouraged to discard things not only before they have been fully used but before they have become intimate and beloved companions of our daily living; and we are induced to believe that most of our mental, emotional, and social problems stem from our lack of the right material goods.

It makes us want things for the wrong reasons. The easiest emotions for the advertiser to tap—and the ones most certain to produce "results"—are those related to our fears, particularly our social fears; our hunger for attention and prestige; and our frustration-born pleasure in outdoing somebody else. These are not our most mature emotions—nor those most conducive to our further maturing. They all represent in some degree an immature centering upon the self. The fears, for example, that advertisers most effectively capitalize—even when they are directing their appeals at grown men and women—are adolescent fears: fears that have to do with being "different," with failing to meet rigid standards of group conformity, with being left out, with not making a good appearance, with being criticized by other people. Similarly, their prestige-appeals are largely on the adolescent level: the individual is invited to see himself, not as maturely equal with others, but *as the focus of attention and envy.*

Advertising, in brief, like the other businesses we have been weighing, has found its formula: get a person to want something for himself, and to want it badly enough, and a sale is made. The art of salesmanship—and therefore of advertising—is that of awakening self-wants: making the person feel that his own life is incomplete and that what it lacks wears a price-tag. The perfect consumer is the individual who is so suggestible that he can be kept pretty continuously engaged in the process of indulging his own ego. If the proper maturing of the self consists, as we have seen, in its development away from immature fears and egocentricities toward a wider range of human interests and relationships, then the ego-absorptions encouraged by endless invitations to buy actually arrest our maturing. Advertising has its own peculiar vested interest: in human self-indulgence.

We speak of ours as a materialistic age—and thus throw

upon material goods an onus they do not deserve. It would be less ambiguous to call it a self-indulgent age. The most powerful forces around us beg us, implore us, plead with us to indulge ourselves. We hear the insinuating words on the radio: "You owe it to yourself . . ."; "Don't wait another day . . ."; "Be the first in your town to own . . ."; "Your friends will envy you. . . ." We read the words of persuasion in flaring spreads in newspapers, in magazine pictures that invite us to project ourselves into a dream-world of beauty and convenience, in neon signs against the night sky: something to drink; something to smoke; something to eat that champions eat; something to make you beautiful; something to make you a man of distinction; something to bring you success; something to make you the life of the party; something to reduce some kind of work to the mere pushing of a button; something to take away all your worries and let you lie in a hammock the rest of your life.

VI

Newspapers, radio, movies, and advertising—these might be called the "big four" of communication. These are the four great money-making enterprises of mind-making. It would be pleasant to report that they all make for the fine maturing of human character. But the report must be otherwise. In spite of what each has contributed to our growth, each has, through its own formula, found it profitable to keep us from full psychological maturing. Or, to put the best possible face upon the matter, each has found in us some immaturity that waited to be tapped. Engaged in the tapping process, each of these powerful forces has been too busy to think about the long-range consequences of its formula.

Lest we be tempted, however, to pass the buck to these great agencies of influence—laying on them the total blame for our immaturity—three final observations must be made.

The first is that the owners and producers of newspapers, radio programs, motion pictures, and advertisements are not to be regarded in their money-making preoccupation, as cultural "sports." Their values are not atypical; they are typical. The definitions of prestige and success that they emphasize are the definitions to which most men and women, right down the line, gear their lives and the lives of their children. The hunger for "shock news"—catastrophe, scandal, conflict —that newspapers satisfy to their own profit is not a newspaper-made hunger, though it may be a newspaper-stimulated hunger. It derives from deeper ills in our culture: from boredoms, disappointments, and apathies that make adults, by and large, unresponsive to any drama in life except "shock drama"; also, from latent hostilities that make adults, by and large, draw guilty satisfaction from the ill fortunes of others. The propensity to daydream that has proved so vastly profitable to the producers of soap operas, motion pictures, and glamor advertisements is, again, stimulated by, but not created by, those who thus make money from its existence. In a culture where everyone is encouraged to believe, at the outset, that his ship will come in and where this hope is so regularly flouted; and in a culture where love and marriage are so constantly presented as adolescent affairs of everlasting moonlight and roses, the frustration of people is enormous—and their propensity to daydream is likewise enormous. While, therefore, we have every right to look at these powerful mind-makers with critical eyes, seeing how ready they are to capitalize our immaturities, we need also to look beyond them for the causes of those immaturities they capitalize.

The second observation that must be made is that these mind-makers are not as dangerous to human welfare as they might be. That statement sounds like bland dismissal of our problem; but it is, rather, a simple recognition of fact. Everywhere in the world, and in every period of history, the job of mind-making has been in large measure the monopoly of some power group or groups. Nowhere in the world, and at no time in history, has the average man actually "made up his own mind." Priests and theologians have made it up for him. Kings have made it up for him. Conquerors dictators, and politicians have made it up for him. While his own personal experience has taught him much, his basic beliefs about his rights and obligations and his place in the scheme of things have come to him from the outside. Always there have been some few—seers, prophets, teachers, statesmen— who have wanted him to think well of himself as a human being and to act out a proud, creative role in the human tradition. But for the most part, everywhere and always, the dominant power group has wanted the average man to have an image of himself that would comport well with the power and perpetuation of that group. Newspaper owners, advertisers, and the rest, when they are persuading the average man to see himself in a role that is profitable to them, are therefore, we might say, simply the inheritors of age-old power techniques and power-attitudes. They—like uncounted priests, demagogues, and dictators before them—are simply mind-making to their own advantage. But that tells only half the story. Psychologically, the most dangerous power-groups and power-individuals in history have been those who have wanted the average man to be *a contented follower:* a meek accepter of his lot; a proud borrower of significance from the leader he served. The four great mind-making powers of our day are less concerned with the average man as *a contented follower* than they are with him as *a discontented wanter of things for himself.* They do not, in the traditional sense, see him as a follower at all. They see him as a consumer. This is a fundamental difference. It means that they will provide whatever that average man—writ large to make a public—is ready to want to pay for. They have modified the old utilitarian slogan—*the greatest good of the greatest number*—to read *the greatest amount of goods to the greatest number.* They may, through their reliance upon their immature formulae, delay the maturing of the public. But their aim is to make money, not to see themselves as "leaders" to whom the passive millions lift adoring eyes. Every cubit of maturity that is added, through whatever influence, to our cultural stature will, therefore, influence the quality of the products put at our disposal by the great mind-makers. If and when we want maturity, in brief, they will cater as assiduously to our mature wants as they now do to our immaturity.

The third observation is that there are ways in which the

public can learn to handle even immature materials maturely. There are high schools, for example, today, in which the students are learning to work up their own standards of criticism for motion pictures and radio programs—and are, in the process, maturing their own powers of discrimination. There are high-school and college classes in increasing numbers in which students are comparing various newspapers and magazines and are trying to decide upon standards of measurement. There are parent groups, small and large, that are taking collective issue with the assumption that any motion picture is good enough so long as it will keep their children out of the house and off the street for a few hours. Similarly, there are parent groups that are coming to joint decisions about the radio programs to which their children of various age levels should listen. The growth of consumer groups is another evidence that the public can learn to be something more mature than the advertiser's "perfect consumer." Such methods for making demands upon those who make our minds are in their infancy. But it is a promising infancy. It offers hope that the time will come in our culture when newspapers, radio stations, motion-picture producers, and advertisers may all find it profitable to appeal to our maturity.

TEN

THE HOME AS A PLACE FOR GROWING

THE ARRESTING and somewhat terrifying fact about the home is that in it new human beings are wholly at the disposal of the old. The child may come trailing clouds of glory; but what happens to these largely depends upon the adults who have the child in their control: who both lay down the initial rules for his behavior and build his first expectations about life.

No social institution is more fateful for the human race than the home. In it the primary shaping of character takes place. In a good home, maturing gets quickly under way: the child is helped to grow from stage to stage of confidence, skill, affection, responsibility, and understanding. The "light of common day" into which he grows has its own permanent radiance: it does not dissipate his clouds of glory. In a bad home, maturing is variously arrested: the child is made to feel unwanted, perhaps, so that he cannot move confidently into life; or he is terrified by threats, so that he shies away from life; or he is kept nervously on edge by erratic adult moods that he can never learn to predict; or he is made the object of jealous competition between the parents; or he is forced to get everything he needs by such aggressive competition with other children that the word "enemy" soon has more meaning for him than the word "friend"; or he is distorted in his attitudes toward other people by the contagious prejudices of his elders; or he is introduced early, again by contagion, to the belief that life has no meaning beyond the scramble to get the necessities.

If homes are psychologically sound, there is hope for our culture. If homes are psychologically unsound there is little hope; for in that case those who are born into those homes will merely grow from childhood into adulthood, not from immaturity into maturity. This puts upon all adults who create homes a large measure of responsibility for determining what our culture and the world culture is to be.

Also, however, it works the other way around: not only is the home a chief creator of maturity or immaturity in our society; but society is a chief creator of maturity or immaturity in the home. For the adults who establish a home were themselves conditioned, not only by their own long-ago childhood, but by all the institutions outside the home that have shaped them and laid requirements upon them. The institutions of industry, business, education, government, and religion go far toward determining the type of institution that the home can be.

We have, therefore, two inquiries to make: one, into the maturity level of those adults who, in the homes of our culture, create the growth-environment of the young; the other, into the effect that the major institutions of our culture have upon the home. Here, we shall make the second inquiry first.

II

It is obvious that institutions other than the home are accountable for much that is good and bad within the home. Economic forces that keep homes insecure and that may even destroy them; community forces that breed antagonisms and group tensions; schools of the type that perpetuate various ignorances, snobbishnesses, and emotional provincialisms; churches of the type that generate intolerance; political forces that breed corruption and war—all these may be so powerful that individual fathers and mothers, however mature, may be helpless to counter them. Neither depression nor war, we are coming to realize, singles out for attack only those homes in which the parents are doing a poor job of bringing up their children. Before we place a full measure of responsibility upon parents, therefore, we need to determine the extent to which the institutions of our society are responsible for our homes.

The American home is not something eternal and unchanging. It is the recent product of a recently developed industrial culture. In one respect, of course, it is something eternal and unchanging: it is, as homes have always been in our Western culture, the place where children are born and reared; and to this extent it is part of a tradition that traces back through the centuries. Yet in its specific structure the American home today is largely the product of the Industrial Revolution of yesterday.

The coming of steam-driven machinery worked a basic change in the home. In fact, that historic event presents us with a significant example of how helpless individual parents can be in the face of powerful social forces. Once the Industrial Revolution was in full swing, no amount of individual resistance to what machinery was doing to the home could have prevented the machinery from doing precisely what it did. The machine age made, among its other products, a machine-age home. It is that machine-age home—not the home typical of the pre-industrial period—that must now find its way to mature happiness both in spite of and in co-operation with the industrial forces that play upon it.

The chief maturity-problem of our time is to discover how the home, under difficult and often forbidding conditions, can provide the experiences that will encourage the continuance of psychological growth from infancy through adulthood. We well know what some of the difficult conditions are. The machine has built the city; the city, in turn, has condemned most families to live in spaces so small that it is hard in the extreme for individuals to find a full release for their creative powers. There is not enough privacy. There is not enough silence; and yet there are not enough places in which children can make the legitimate noises of childhood without being shushed and hushed. There are, from the point of view of children's maturing, too many automatic buttons to push.and too few raw materials on which to try their ingenuity. There are too few chores suitable to different levels of growth: chores that are not "made work," but that actually must be done for the common welfare and that make each child a useful part of the total family. There are too few growing things with which the child can become intimate and from which he can learn the ways of natural growth: too few pets; too few places of planting and harvest.

Again, the machine age in creating the city has made the home into a place chiefly surrounded by strangers. Where the overwhelming majority of the human beings whom children see are total strangers, whose problems they will never know and whose skills and kindnesses they will never have a chance to appreciate, parents are hard put to it to encourage either the simple arts of neighboring or the more complex arts of community.

Again, within the home itself, the machine age has wrought changes of dubious import. On the one hand, it has brought the mother too close to the children as a dominant psychological force. On the other hand, it has taken the father too far away from them.

In the small spaces of the modern home, the mother is kept stiflingly close to the young during their first formative months and years. She cannot let the toddler out of her sight when the only place for him to go is a city street. She has no one except an occasional hired "sitter" with whom to leave the little ones during her absences. Under these conditions, the attitude of the mother toward her children tends to become one of either irritation or over-solicitude—this latter often masking an unconscious and guilty resentment, or an exaggerated need to make her own sense of significance out of the children's reliance upon her. The attitude of the children toward the mother becomes, in turn, all too often, one of unhealthy prolonged dependence—and of open or repressed hostility, because prolonged dependence is recognized, in the child's unconscious, as a threat to its ego.

Fathers, on the other hand, have been forced by the economic requirements of modern life to spend most of the waking hours of most of their days away from home—and therefore away from their children. Instead of being continuous forces in their children's lives, influencing them by the contagion of their work and by their comments upon the affairs of home and work, fathers have come to occupy an anomalous position. It might almost be said that, in relation to the home, the father is something between an absentee owner and a house guest. He earns a living for the family, but by mysterious processes that the children only vaguely understand. He is "head of the family," but most decisions are left to the mother because he does not want to be bothered with them "at the end of a hard day's work." Such "under-fathering" is not good for children. It makes it altogether too difficult for them to build, gradually and normally, an image of adequate masculine adulthood.

Fathers and mothers—and therefore, children—are victims of an age that has built its factories and offices without taking account of what these were doing to the home. The result is that in countless homes, today, the major condition for the maturing of the young—namely, wholesome dependable contact with mature adults of both sexes—is too rarely realized.

Another thing has happened. Large families have become rare. This, too, has important bearings upon the problem of maturity. One way in which children have traditionally turned their feeling of helplessness into a feeling of strength has been through the group solidarity of the young. Children have shared their secrets with one another, have contrived their own private language, have by their signs and symbols made a world that adults could not invade. When they have experienced injustice, they have been able to confide in one another. They have been able to share with one another their conviction that grownups are a silly lot terribly concerned with things that do not matter. They have been able to work off their hard feelings toward their parents by talking together and planning small revenges. Thus, even though adults have been in command, there has been, traditionally, a kind of community of childhood. While this community has never seriously challenged adult authority, it has given children a certain sense of having a world of their own—a world of companionship in which to learn the ways of equality; a world in which they could make rules which, from their point of view, have made sense.

The larger the number of children in a home the more effective the community of children is likely to be. While they will, on occasion, have feuds among themselves and form subgroups of companionship, each child—where there are a number—is likely to have someone to be with in time of need. Also, the larger the number of children the less intense is likely to be the competition for adult notice and affection.

Where there is only one child, that child is perilously dominated by the adult pattern. Where there are only two, the advantage of companionship is often neutralized by the disadvantage of keen competition for parental approval—for individual differences stand out in stark relief; and any attention shown to one child easily looks like neglect of the other. This is one reason, we might note in passing, why nursery schools and kindergartens are such essential institutions in an age of small families. They provide a community of childhood where such a community is lacking in the home. In some degree at least they save children from the isolation they might otherwise experience within a world overpoweringly adult.

The change to the small family pattern has serious psychological implications. Growth into maturity requires growth into self-confidence. It requires, also, growth into the arts of companionship. It requires the experience of understanding other persons—playing with them, working with them, helping them in time of need, making shared plans with them. In the one-child or two-child family, the conditions for such growth are hard to provide. Tentative self-confidence is easily shattered in a child by the overmastering pattern of adult requirements. A companionship of sharing is difficult between parents and children: the age-gap is too great; the difference in actual authority makes the pretense of equality ring false. The greatly maturing experience of helping others in time of need can rarely be had by a child whose chief associates are adults. He does not understand their problems as he would understand those of other children; the things he can do are too small in comparison to the size of their needs; their worries, when they infect the home atmosphere, make him feel so insecure by contagion that his own emotions become a problem that shuts out a larger view.

III

Thus, many things have happened to the home since machinery entered the world. For the most part, these things have not been clearly recognized by the individuals involved. The average adult, even the average parent, takes the home for granted as if it had come in its present form straight from the workshop of the Creator. Any suggestion that many things need to be changed, particularly in the economic order that has been so largely responsible for the altered and insecure modern home, either leaves him unconvinced or rouses him to anger against "radicalism." This is in itself a sign of adult immaturity. The very institution the adult most cares about is one about which he knows so little—and thinks so little, in any deep sense—that he has allowed it to become an institution secondary in power and at the mercy of forces that he considers it un-American to try to change.

It is quite possible that most of what has happened to the home is still beyond our individual power to correct. But maturity of mind would seem to require at least some intelligent awareness of the situation. The home is not the perfect institution that immature sentimentality makes it out to be. It is, today, full of serious dangers to the psychological health of both its individual members and our total culture. A readiness to see these dangers is called for—and an awareness of their character. The mature adult will regard the modern home as something to be deeply anxious about. Also, he will regard it as something to be cherished—and changed.

IV

Within this imperfect institution—this product of socioeconomic forces still largely beyond our control—there are many things that lie within our control. Fundamentally, we ourselves have it within our power as makers of a home to be either growing or fixated.

If children are to mature, they must grow into all the basic linkages with life that we have already described. Whether they do thus grow will largely depend upon whether the adults in the home have themselves formed and are continuing to strengthen those linkages.

Children must grow from ignorance toward knowledge. If the adults in the home are set in their certainties, intolerant or contemptuous of new insights, too bigoted or too apathetic to learn, they will provide a poor climate for the growth of young minds. It cannot be said too often that children learn chiefly by contagion. Where adults are complacent in ignorance, children tend to look upon learning as one more of the inexplicable tasks wished upon them by arbitrary adults. On the other hand, where adults are eager about the things of the mind, children are helped toward a lifetime of comparable eagerness.

Children must grow from irresponsibility to responsibility. Here again the adult must put the test to himself. Has he become fixated within so narrow and repetitive a range of responsibilities that his children will come to identify responsibility with dull routine? Even within that narrow range, does he carry his responsibilities grudgingly? Or is he still growing—and happily growing—in his sense of what the wide human fellowship requires of him? Does he, by contagion, make it seem a privilege to be able to contribute to the common good?

Telling children that they "ought" to do certain things is no more than an exercise of arbitrary power unless those who lay down the rules accept with good grace the things that they themselves ought to do; unless, in brief, they make the province of adult responsibility seem a good one toward which to grow. Parents who understand this fact understand also that the home offers them countless chances to invite the children to join in responsible experience. They look upon the home as a place where each individual child can learn to enjoy participating in a common family enterprise; where each will grow, in mind as well as body, beyond dependent babyhood toward self-reliance, skill, and generous contribution.

Children must grow from verbal isolation into communication. Here, once more, the test must first be put to the father and mother who are the children's most influential companions and pace-setters. Are they mature—and still maturing—in their communicative habits and skills? Can they say what they mean with some degree of accuracy? Can they help others to say what they mean? Does their way of talking give the impression that life is wholly an experience of monotones; or an experience of pomposity; or an experience of self-pity? Or do they, through their words and inflections, convey the feeling that life has range, that it holds wonder as well as conviction, intense caring as well as casualness, and joy and sorrow in normal amounts? Adults who speak only to deliver the final word of truth and authority are no fit companions for children. Neither are adults who are grumpy in their uncommunicativeness. Neither are adults who chatter endlessly about the trivial.

The home can be an ever-available laboratory for the development of gracious and intelligent communication. This is no small function for the home to perform. Far too many of the evils and the lonelinesses of life arise out of man's misunderstanding of man. In most homes there is no conversation; there are only competitive monologues of gossip, complaint, or command.

Children must grow toward sexual maturity. The scandal of most homes, if we would recognize it as such, is that the adults in them are not themselves sexually mature.

Sex is for them, all too often, a hush-hush affair, an ugliness, an indelicacy, a thing of shame. Before any mention of it, they catch their breath nervously—like primitives in the presence of a taboo. They find it impossible, therefore, to put their children on honest good terms with their own bodies and their own emotions. They blush, stammer, put off the day when they must explain to those children "the facts of life"—as though sexual facts were somehow divorced from all others that have to do with the how of things.

Or sex is for them a channel for the release of their own emotional immaturities. Family life is too often made to seem a battle of the sexes. The father tells his son that all men, sooner or later, get trapped by some woman; but he neglects to say that the reason he feels trapped is that he has never actually wanted to take on adult responsibilities—that, emotionally, he would have preferred to remain a dependent child or a flitting adolescent. The mother tells her daughter never to trust any man too far: "They're all alike." She neglects to say that she has always envied men their role in a "man's world"; or that she finds in sex antagonism a handy outlet for her general hostility toward life; or that her own romantic illusions about marriage were such that even the best husband on earth would have cut a poor figure when compared with her "Prince Charming."

Where adults are sexually mature—that is, creatively happy in their shared sex life—the home becomes a place where the radiance of their maturity is in contagious evidence. In such a home, children are not likely to develop those resistances to sexual knowledge, those morbid misconceptions, or those shallow excitements that make sex, in so many lives, a dirty and ugly burden to carry. Instead, they are likely to learn that sexual experience is a rich part of a rich companionship: that shared bodily joy, a mutual affirmation of personalities, and a joint creative planning all go into the making of a marriage.

Children must grow away from their native egocentricity.
Once more the first responsibility lies with the parents. The
home can be an almost perfect place for helping the child
to get his own ego out of the center. In innumerable ways,
he can there be led to take an interest in lives beyond his
own: through the care he gives his pets; through his chances
to make things grow and to love them in their growing;
through consideration for older people and for children
smaller than himself; through common courtesies; through
sharing what is his with other children; through such simple
practices as the writing of letters or the remembering of
people's birthdays. But the child will not thus grow beyond
his own small egocentricities unless his mother and father
have, in some fair measure, grown beyond theirs. To be sure,
nature seems sometimes to have ways of triumphing that
are not on the books of logic and out of selfish parents will
contrive a generous child. But it is best not to put too great
a strain on nature's ingenuity. On no count are ego-centered
parents the best influence for helping children to grow beyond their ego-absorptions. Affection calls forth affection;
empathy calls forth empathy; consideration calls forth consideration; an out-reaching adult interest in human happiness
communicates itself from parent to child.

Finally, *children must grow out of particular seeing into
whole-seeing.* They must learn the way of the philosophic
mind. In the home, from the very beginning of his life, the
child should be learning the delight and power of seeing
things in their wider relationships. But here, as before, the
pointing is to the adult. Is he mature in his sense of how things

hang together? Is he competent to see significances beyond the obvious, to see the unlabeled characteristics of people and things, and to awaken in his children an interest in meanings? Or does he nose into life like a mole, seeing neither to right nor to left, but blindly burrowing in a mental and spiritual darkness? If so, the wisdom he thinks he possesses is likely to prove a foolishness visted upon his children to the third and fourth generation.

V

The home is a place for growing. It is, therefore, imperatively a place where adults must themselves be growing and where there is some knowledge of how growth is accomplished. It is no place for adults who are unwilling, in pride or apathy, to learn and to keep learning about the peculiar ways of human growth. Again, it must be a place where all that the parents can learn about psychological growth, as well as physical, is given a daily workout in practice. Finally, the home is a place where we can begin to remake our culture. If our culture has slipped into unsound habits of irresponsibility and egocentricity, the home is a place where we can begin to mitigate these habits. If our culture has slipped into carelessness regarding human values, the home is a place where those values can be cherished and made to grow in influence. If our culture has learned to put a disastrously high premium on competition, the home is a place where the co-operative arts can be a strength and a delight.

Nowhere in our culture is there an institution that can,

more variously and deeply, serve the needs of our maturing than can the home. Even in a world where economic and political forces, and often educational and religious forces as well, are dangerously immature, the home can be made into a place where, from childhood on, we learn not only the ways but the rewards of genuine maturity.

ELEVEN

EDUCATION: A QUESTION MARK

SCHOOLS ARE an anomaly. They are designed to do
two things: to pass on the culture and to help the young
to grow into their adult role. Without changing a word in
that second sentence, we can apply it to our worst and our
best schools. A school can pass on the culture and help the
student to find his adult role—and can end up by making
him a complete reactionary and a routineer. Or it can pass
on the culture and help the student to find his adult role in
such a way that he becomes a liberal-minded co-creator of
man's future and a person of unique powers. It is this fact—
namely, that the function assigned to schools permits them
to do such widely different things—that makes education
such a challenging problem.

From the point of view of helping the young to mature,
schools ought to be of the second sort. Far too often they
are not—and the reason is not surprising. As public institu-

tions, schools reflect the public. If, as we have seen, that public has stopped short of full psychological maturity, it is to be expected that the educational system will likewise have stopped short.

In the first place, schools are governed by school boards. These boards are made up of average adults brought up on the average interpretations of our culture. They are not likely to be happy in the thought of turning the schools into experimental stations or into places where the young will learn to look with measuring eyes at the *status quo*. Most board members have relatively fixed attitudes in economic, political, and social matters. These attitudes seem to them, not only reasonable, but the only ones that are reasonable— and this in spite of the fact that they may be far from mature. All attitudes that have antedated their own in history are proved unreasonable by the fact that they have become out-moded. All that are contemporary with their own, but representative of other cultures, are "backward." All that look to a different future—unless couched as remote ideals for which the time is not ripe—offer, somehow, a threat to their own habits and prestige-pattern, and seem therefore to be either foolish or dangerous. In all sincerity, they come to the conclusion that those schools will best perform their rightful task which turn out students with attitudes like their own.

Few kings in history have willingly abdicated to make way for a system different from their own. The psychological principle back of this fact can be broadly applied: few people who have come to any position of authority and prestige, however small it may be, willingly abdicate in favor of a new regime; and the vast majority of those who tenaciously hold on to positions of power do so believing that they are defending the right and the reasonable. There has been nothing in their own experience of success—and therefore their experience of satisfaction—to make them see as inadequate that by which they have succeeded. School board members, by and large, are among the many human beings who demonstrate the workings of this psychological principle. To the extent that they are mentally, emotionally, and socially immature in a culture where they can find ample support for their immaturity, the schools will tend to be immature in like fashion. This is almost a foregone conclusion.

In the second place, schools are staffed by teachers and administrators who, in large numbers, have come out of immature homes, schools, and colleges. Also, these teachers and administrators—like the rest of us—are daily and hourly played upon by all the various institutions, economic, political, journalistic, and otherwise, that have become arrested short of full social maturity. The fact that these individuals are "educators" neither makes them immune to the pressures to which the rest of us variously yield nor effects in them any sudden transformation from what they have been made by past pressures. For the most part, they remain as much the products of cultural conditioning as the rest of us; and they proceed to pass on the immature factors of their conditioning not one whit less honestly and industriously than the mature factors.

It is not surprising, then, that in the average school, students are insidiously led to believe that the mature art of thinking for themselves is "dangerous." It is dangerous so far as their own prospects are concerned: for who is going to want to hire a young person who is known to be "different" or "radical"? It is dangerous, also, they are persuaded, so far as the future of our American way of life is concerned: for how can it be other than dangerous to tamper with the excellent, or to substitute the untried for the tried?

Students, naturally, are taught to think *within limits*. The outstanding characteristic of average education is that these limits to thought are not talked about; they are fixed *by the lessons assigned*. Students are required to know what their textbooks and teachers tell them. They are not exposed to other materials that might move them to new doubts and curiosities. If they did happen upon these materials, there would be no scholastic profit to be derived from studying them; there would be no occasion for handing them back to the teacher. They belong to some order of being that is not that of the curriculum. When students know enough of what their textbooks and teachers have told them, they are supposedly ready to go forth into life.

This is indeed one way of passing on the traditions of a culture and preparing a student for an adult role—if that role is conceived as one of simply "fitting in." But if the adult role is more maturely conceived as one of confronting the culture and creatively helping it to grow into its future stages, then the schools, for the most part, prepare badly for this role. Right preparation for it would require, from the outset, a different attitude. It would require an exploratory and creative attitude toward life. It would ask that children be encouraged to develop inquiring minds rather than merely acceptive and reproducing minds; critical minds rather than merely passive and credulous.

Only rare schools build minds in this sense; for the most part, they build mental adding machines. Fact is added to fact, until the sum of the facts is equal to graduation. Seldom is the power developed in students to do an independent job of relating fact to fact, of interpreting and evaluating them, and of exploring where they lead. The major pressure put upon most students is to accumulate and store up facts that are already known to their teachers and the authors of their textbooks.

I I

I have no wish to exaggerate. The classroom processes in the schools of America seem so earnestly concerned about encouraging the minds of the young that the foregoing strictures may seem unjust. Within limits, it must be said again, minds *are* made to function. Children learn, after a fashion, to read and write; to spell; to add, subtract, multiply, and divide; to recite facts of geography, history, and science. They learn facts about economics, politics, and civics; facts about their bodily processes. All these are useful, but, as taught in the average school, they come far short of building minds capable, in the end, of undertaking a mature, creative, responsible adult role.

A mature adult role, properly speaking, can never be one of passive and uncritical acceptance. It must be one of creative evaluation. The mature adult is a thinking adult. He is an adult who meditates values, considers the bearings of things, tries to foresee consequences, tries to get rid as best he can of "the personal equation" that makes him see what his fears and hopes tell him to see, imagines better ways of doing things. A mature adult, in brief, is a mind actively confronting life and trying to do what needs to be done to improve the life-situation.

The schools could take upon themselves no more significant task than to prepare the young to become mature adults. If they were to adopt this function, however, they might have to adopt also a new educational commandment: Seek first the building of a *mind*.

The building of a mind can begin in earliest childhood and can continue throughout all the young years. It requires simply that we accept the fact that a mind functions when it makes its independent estimate of things; draws its own conclusions. Learning that two plus two equals four does not actually involve the functioning of the mind, but merely of that ready servant of the mind, the memory. Most of what we have been accustomed to call education has been chiefly an enlisting of the memory. Building a mind means confronting it with problems to be solved; letting it search out the relevant evidence; letting it learn to weigh this evidence, come to a conclusion, and test that conclusion. The whole process is worlds apart from the mere acceptance of statements on the say-so of textbook and teacher.

The important thing here is the building of a right mental habit. The habit of uncritical credulity—of taking what the

textbook or the teacher says and handing it back for approval
—encourages a character structure apt at ways of dependence and dogmatism. On the other hand, the habit of seeking
for evidence, weighing it, arriving carefully—even prayer-
fully—at a conclusion leads to a character structure that is
modest in the face of life's complexities, honest and self-
reliant in searching out facts, and undogmatic in assertion.
The first exhibits the immaturity of a dependent child; the
second, the maturity of a self-reliant, grown-up mind.

As we have said, the mind's maturing can begin even in
earliest childhood. I remember how one kindergarten teacher,
for example, developed in the children a thinking approach
to "laws." She did not simply tell them, on the authority of
her teacherhood, that laws were laws, necessary for living,
and that they had to be obeyed. She let them find this out
for themselves. Were there any rules, she asked, in the school?
What were they? "Mustn't run on the stairs," one child said.
"Why do we have that rule?" "Because running on stairs is
dangerous to the other children." Another child gave the
rule for helping when some child spilled its milk: the child
next to it was to help wipe up; others were to stay in their
places. Again, the relevant reasons for such a rule were
sought out.

Here was one way of helping children to make mature
responses to situations on their own level of experience.
This, in fact, is the clue to all mind-building in children:
find the problem-situations that are real *to them* and let them
work out the solutions. The time will come, as children grow,
when many of our most perplexing social problems will be-

come real to them: problems that adults may not yet have solved—of labor and capital, sex, divorce, politics, and war. Schools that take seriously the commandment to seek first the building of a mind will not, at any point along the line, change their approach and demand the acceptance of fixed answers. They will realize that neither the avoiding of issues nor the handing out of pat answers will build minds— though these processes may satisfy a timid public or time-serving politicians. Educators who believe that the maturing of the mind is the central function of the schools will not want students simply to become like their elders. They will not, therefore, desert those students at the stage of their development where social problems begin to feel like personal problems.

I remember one notable instance in which the courage of a high-school teacher was dramatically justified. A teacher of the social sciences, he let his students range freely among the controversial problems that were becoming real to their consciousness. But he insisted that they approach each problem with utmost honesty and rigor of mind, searching out the evidence and coming to considered conclusions. The expected thing happened. The students talked at home. Parents became anxious. Their boys and girls were being turned into radicals. They wrote letters to the principal demanding that this dangerous teacher be dismissed.

The principal was wise. He showed the letters to the teacher, and between them they devised an experiment. The teacher invited a few of the parents to a social evening at his home. Instead of letting the talk run aimlessly on, he nudged it into a channel that led to a discussion of a current controversial issue. Carefully and wisely, then, he drew out reasons for opposing views, keeping the discussion free of vituperative emotion. So good a time was had that his guests asked for more such meetings. Finally, after a number of similar evenings in the teacher's home, when they had learned to like the process of bringing relevant facts out into the open and giving them their due weight, they asked that other parents be given a like experience. Out of the suggestion came a community forum which became notable for the completely free discussion of all sides of questions. Thereafter, there were no more parental demands that teachers be dismissed for encouraging an honest classroom-confronting of social issues.

Until minds learn how to think, and are given full encouragement to think, there can hardly be mature character structure.

III

For schools to stimulate thought is, then, the basic requirement. But other important things need to follow: three in particular.

In the first place, schools are in a position to help build in the young the indispensable habit of co-operation. The traditional school did not concern itself with this habit. Children co-operated in their play, at recess time, but in the classroom competition for marks was the rule—so much the rule that the ambitious child could hope that others would fail and that he alone could give the right answer. In many ways, this is changing. The significance of the "project method" lies precisely here: it means the enlisting of children in a common enterprise, so that the success of each is the success of all, and the failure of each the failure of all. For this reason it is a maturing method; through it children and adolescents learn to pool their insights and energies, to work for common ends, and to take stock of such individual habits and attitudes as make or break the co-operative enterprise.

Schools cannot advance far beyond the culture that contains them. But in that culture, after all, there are two major strains of philosophy and practice: the competitive and the co-operative. In order to help bring about a new maturing of their students—and eventually of their culture—schools need only emphasize the cultural strain that they have hitherto largely neglected: the co-operative.

In the second place, schools can help to build in the young the habit of civic obligation. The traditional thing has been for youngsters to study in school a kind of "civics" that they will eventually, it is presumed, practice as adults: that they will practice chiefly by casting a vote. Educators are beginning to realize, however, that this implies too narrow a meaning for the word "civic." Properly speaking, "civic" has to do with all the things that pertain to people's living together in a community. Children, no less than adults, live in a community: of the home, the school, and the town or city that contains the school. A civic character structure is one that recognizes community obligations and faithfully carries them out.

If schools have largely failed to develop civic character in their students, it has been because they have unwittingly kept them in the role of civic dependents. All responsibility for the physical environment—its care, beauty, cleanliness, and sanitation—has been relegated to grown-ups: teachers, administrators, custodians. Similarly, responsibility for the school's psychological well-being—orderliness, honesty, friendliness, attention to work—has been relegated to teachers and administrators. Students, in short, have learned the dependent habit of living in a school community with whose arrangements and government they have nothing whatever to do. Expected later to behave as free and responsible citizens, they are allowed, through most of their young years, to grow up without developing any basic habits of citizen interest and citizen participation.

The young who go to school also live in the community that contains the schools. They walk the streets, or bicycle through them, or in their late adolescence drive cars through them. They go to the movies, play games in the parks, swim in the pools or at the beaches, meet in couples and crowds at the soda fountain. In all these activities they are linked with the life of the community—by their considerateness or their lack of it, their sense of responsibility or their lack of it. If they make intolerable nuisances of themselves, their failure is a *civic* failure. It is as irresponsible *citizens* that they disturb the audience in a motion-picture theater with their noisy roughhousing; that they litter up the parks; that they defile swimming pools and beaches.

In a few schools throughout the nation—so few that they still stand out as surprising exceptions—educators have realized that students will not achieve civic maturity by being treated as civic dependents. If they are to grow up as members of a community, they must be self-governing members of that community that is peculiarly theirs: the school. They must be helped to think through all the relationships that exist within this community and to organize themselves into self-governing bodies for dealing with all the problems that have to do with the fulfillment of these relationships. They must be helped, moreover, to take on civic obligations in the larger community that contains the school. Civic maturity does not come by magic nor by the grace of some certain day on the calendar. It comes by civic experience. One major task of the schools is to provide occasion for that experience.

Finally, the schools can build in the young a creative approach to life. Growth toward maturity is a growth away from the automatic and the imitative. A mature person is one who sees with his own eyes, thinks with his own brain, and creates with his own ingenuity and his own sense of values.

Only in recent years have schools been recognized as places where the creative powers of children are to be encouraged into growth. In the traditional school, children did things by "rote." In many of our best schools, today, there is a new generous understanding of what child life has in it to be. In these schools, children are helped to approach maturity along avenues of creative interest.

The rote-taught child, we are coming to realize, grows into the routine-bound adult—unconscious of whole areas of human power and interest; unskilled in self-entertainment; dependent upon the ready-made; clumsy with the materials out of which he might have learned to fashion beauty and significance. If most adults can properly be called "adulleds" it is largely because most schools, in the past, have failed to open up to students the amazing resources of human appreciation and creation.

I V

The schools remain an anomaly. They are anything, and they can be everything. Their chief failure, perhaps, has lain in the fact that they have not known their rightful function.

They have tried to pass on the culture to successive new generations; but they have seldom seen the culture they are trying to pass on with a vivid enough sense of what it has meant. They have located its heroisms in the past. They have located in the past its struggles for freedom and abundance of life. In the present, they are seeing it chiefly in terms of order and the security of the familiar. Following the safe ways of conservatism, they have forgotten that the very essence of our democratic culture has been a revolt against the inadequate and the outworn.

They have, again, tried to prepare children for their adult role; but they have seldom recognized that role in its full maturity. They have judged adulthood by its current manifestations of social timidity, self-interest, and acquisitiveness; hence, they have felt that young people have been learning their proper role when they have been learning to fit in and not to ask too much of life.

Few schools have yet recognized that their central function is that of helping young life to grow into mental, emotional, and social maturity. This recognition must come as our next great educational adventure. Everywhere there are signs that the new imperative is being heeded. Teachers, administrators, and an increasing public begin to catch onto the fact that our old concept of adulthood is not good enough; that a new concept of maturity must take its place; and that the only adequate education, therefore, must be one that encourages the immature to become mature.

"Out of fifty years of vigorous thought and experimentation," writes Harold Rugg,[1] "we have come to *conceive the school as an enterprise in living;* hence what was narrowly and forbiddingly called in the old education the curriculum becomes in the new education 'the life and program of the school.' Every aspect of a truly vital education partakes of life itself; the school becomes a school of living . . . learning is seen as living through novel situations . . . the curriculum becomes the very stream of dynamic activities that constitute the life of the young people and their elders. Thus the new school is a social as well as a personal enterprise in living."

In the new school—the school that is on the way to being achieved—the young will be helped to grow day by day into the increasing stature of their personal and social maturity.

[1] *Foundations for American Education,* p. 650. New York, World Book Company.

TWELVE

TOWARD RELIGIOUS MATURITY

IN THE LATE fourth and early fifth centuries A.D., one of the great psychological controversies of all time took place. It had to do with what we should today call the inheritance of acquired psychic characters. Specifically, the question at issue was whether a certain depravity of will that had revealed itself in the adult years of the ancestor of the race was carried by inheritance to all his offspring through all the ages.

One of the parties to the controversy, Pelagius, took the negative. According to his view, Adam's will to disobedience ended where it began. Because, under a momentary temptation, he had misbehaved, there was no reason, Pelagius argued, why every child born thereafter was fated to inherit this same will to misbehavior. Each child in the world, he maintained, starts with his own equipment of powers and carries in him no weight of woe produced by a single ancestral misdemeanor. Augustine, on the contrary, held that Adam's act of disobedience started a long train of psychic inheritance. Every child born thereafter was cursed with the depravity that began with that act of disobedience. Adam's original sin, in short, became a universal and inherent tendency to commit sin. From this tendency the individual could be saved only by Divine favor.

When we think now of the conditions under which this controversy was carried on, we wonder at the deep seriousness with which it was taken—and continues even yet to be taken. There was no attempt at research or rigorous experiment. In fact, Augustine's position was so flagrantly a projection upon the whole human race of his own uncontrollable lusts that a modern psychologist would have thrown out his contentions as untrustworthy and misconceived. Thus the greatest question at issue in our human life—whether we start with powers that enable us fairly well to work out our destiny; or whether, by a mysterious curse, we are defeated at the outset and must appeal to a higher Power to help us out—was settled without the slightest attempt to search for relevant factual evidence. It was settled by sacred writings, by theological disputation, and by theological politics. We might almost say that the curse which, through all subsequent centuries, has rested upon man came, not from Adam, but from Augustine. To a peculiar degree, it was Augustine who denied to our species the healthy blessing of self-respect.

Augustine won this biological-psychological argument, not by decision of a competent body of scientific minds, but chiefly by his power to influence the synods of the Church. He played his Church politics so effectively that Pelagius was declared a heretic.

Did Augustine have the right of the argument? There was nothing in the procedure by which his view was established to make the truth of that view appear so inevitable that an opposite view could only be altogether false. When the rulers of the Church *declared* the Pelagian view a heresy they did not *prove* it to be an error. Yet, once the declaration was made, Augustine's doctrine of original sin became so strongly institutionalized that the question of its truth or falsity virtually ceased to arise. Institutional might made it right.

If the same question were to arise today, it would doubtless be differently handled. In the first place, the "ancestor" would not be a man called Adam but more likely a primordial cell-structure. In the second place, we would look, first of all, for factual evidence. We would not be likely to take as our source authority an ancient, unverifiable creation-tale. Starting thus afresh, we might well conclude that each person comes into the world not only with the traces on him—physical and psychological—of what his ancestors have been and done, but also with his own equipment of powers. No man starts with a biologically and psychologically clean slate. To this extent Augustine was right. On the other hand, no man, so far as we can judge from available evidence, starts life so specifically cursed by a will to evil that he has no chance to direct his powers toward decency and wholeness. To this extent Pelagius was right. The "will to disobedience" that Augustine found in all of us now appears to be merely the

expression of the inevitable conflict between a helpless creature trying to grow into its proper independence and an
environment that the child, in his immaturity, can neither
understand nor master.

The time is at hand to re-view the whole situation. Christian religion as we have known it took over as its own this
premature psychological theory: a theory established long
before there was any equipment of research or experiment
to give it validation. In taking over this premature theory,
Christianity condemned man to a psychological hopelessness
to which Christ himself bore no witness. It declared him to
be basically impotent to work out his psychological salvation.
Instead of encouraging him to develop all the characteristically human powers within him, and so overcome inner
contradictions and outer obstacles, it encouraged him to
distrust himself and malign himself. It encouraged him to
cast himself upon a Power greater than himself—and to
credit, not his own nature, but that mysterious Power, with
every virtue that seemed to reside in his own thoughts and
behaviors. In short, it encouraged the individual to remain a
dependent child.

Much must be attributed to the fact that in Augustine's
day there was not the slightest inkling of what we now understand as the drama of man's maturing. Childhood tempers
and tantrums were seen as evidences of evil will in the child;
stubbornnesses and disobediences as "badnesses" that needed
to be driven out as one would drive out the devil.

At a time when the maturity concept had not yet even
begun to exert its clarifying influence, it is not surprising

that man thus misjudged man. Pelagius was, it would appear, more nearly right than Augustine; but an age that was still in psychological darkness was prepared to accept the easier, because more obvious, view of man's inherent will to evil, rather than the more difficult view of man's inherent power to grow into goodness.

II

What we had from Jesus of Nazareth was an invitation to maturity injected into the immature Roman world. That world could not understand his mature insight. The insight, in fact, so flatly contradicted the going conceptions of that day that those who were bred in those conceptions angrily crucified him.

The Nazarene saw his own people as twice defeated: first, by the brutality of the Roman soldiers and the greedy power of individuals and groups among themselves; second, by their own inability to rise above the success-pattern of those who mastered them. Even the poorest and most wretched among them envied those in power: envied their privileges; admired their exercise of authority; tried to be like them in whatever small way was possible; believed that happiness could come only by the methods the power-people employed. Jesus, with his mature sense of life, tried to get them to see that this was no true way to happiness; that the only true way was a repudiation of the power-pattern. "Blessed are the meek" . . . "He that loseth his life shall find it" . . . "It is more blessed to give than to receive" . . . "Blessed are the peace makers" . . . "Do unto others as ye would that others do unto you." Thus, in multifarious fashion, Jesus shaped an invitation to inner growth. "The kingdom of heaven is within you."

Here was no terrifying reminder to man that he was helpless to save himself because a first ancestor had failed in obedience. Here was a mature man's declaration that the way for a human being to save himself is that of his growing into the fullness of his powers—and into knowledge that the greatest of these powers is love.

If Christian religion could have gone on straight from this point, it would doubtless today be a vastly different thing from what it is. Instead, a few centuries later it was tangled up in a hopeless psychological argument. By some curious quirk of reasoning—and of theological expediency—Adam's disobedience became a more important reality than man's potential love of God and his neighbor.

III

Religion does ill if it clings to old interpretations of human life simply because it has built these into revered institutions and practices. Where a thing as complex and inadequately known as our own nature is being dealt with, there is need for a constant alertness to new discoveries and implications. For this is precisely what man appears to be: *A mind on the way to knowing more than it has known before.* Today, we discover more in ourselves than was hitherto even suspected.

If we were to go freshly at the task of describing the religious way of life, we would now have to start with the concept of man's growth from infancy into adulthood; from

immaturity into maturity; from egocentricity into a socio-
centered linkage with his world. We would have to think
of the individual as moving toward a wholeness of linkages
still impossible to the child and adolescent and not achieved
even by most adults. We would, in short, have to think of
the *movement toward wholeness of linkages* as the essential
thing to care about. Is this child moving *toward* such wholeness or *away from* it? Is he increasing his knowledge, responsibility, affection, and awareness of the wide interrela-
tionships that make all men one in destiny? Or is he sunk
in apathetic ignorance, growing in hatred more than in love,
withdrawing from social responsibilities rather than taking
them on with competent gladness? Is this adolescent, this
adult, moving toward wholeness of linkages?

There ought to be no difficulty in deciding which is the
fulfilling movement of life. Movement toward wholeness of
linkages is precisely *what life is for*. There is nothing else to
be said. This is what Jesus of Nazareth affirmed; this is what
psychologists and psychiatrists are reaffirming. This is what
growth means; what human fulfillment means. "What is the
chief end of man?" To move toward wholeness of life.

IV

In religion, we suffer from an ancient and continuing
indecision. Controversy continues even today over whether
religion comes from a word meaning *taboo,* or from a word,
different by one letter, meaning *to bind together.* Where the
first derivation is accepted, religion is a matter of meticulously
not doing what some Power says we must not do. Religion

of this sort emphasizes the relation of subject to ruler; slave to master; dependent and obedient child to parent. Such religion operates through commands given and received; it approves submission; as rewards for good behavior it gives gifts but never an enlarged freedom. Its basic motivation is fear of the taboo and of the maker of the taboo. "The fear of the Lord is the beginning of wisdom."

The history of Christianity shows this taboo-meaning of religion to have been uppermost in the minds of such leaders as Augustine, Luther, and Calvin. Consequently, since these have been the main architects of the Christian church—Catholic and Protestant—religion as taboo has colored most of our Christian civilization. Such religion has largely operated as an institutionalization of prohibitions and permissions, with fear of punishment and hope of reward as its basic motives.

Taboo religion is addressed to the child-mind. It offers the individual no strong invitation to explore his world, to find out for himself the ways of life that are wise, and to go these ways. It tells the child-mind the things it must do, and warns it of punishments if it does not do these things.

Quite otherwise is the conception that religion means *to bind together*. Paul was describing such "binding" religion when he said, "Religion pure and undefiled is to visit the widows and the fatherless in their affliction and to keep oneself unspotted of the world." To do this meant, in the first place, that one must emerge from childish egocentricity and take an active affectionate interest in the needs of others; and in the second place, that one must refuse to take the world's success-patterns and power-patterns as his own. Jesus communicated such religion when he said, very simply, "Love one another."

Religion in the sense of *binding together* invites man to a mature relationship with life—and therefore, in behalf of that relationship, to a mature development of his own potentialities. The religious life, in this sense, is the one in which there is a constant effort to link oneself, in joy and contribution, to all the life-giving movements of one's world. The religious life, in short, is what we have been describing as the maturing life: it is the maturing life deeply and passionately committed to the search for wholeness.

Today, therefore, religion and psychological science may properly join hands. When it is mature, religion aims at man's maturing. In like manner, psychological science, as it matures, aims at man's maturing.

V

Another episode in religious history bears recalling. When Buddha, the young prince, sorrowed because of the miseries of his fellow men, he was moved to unprecedented action. He started a research into the causes of human misery. Usually this research is reported as a series of marvelous and esoteric tales. But for Buddha it was the effort of a penetrating mind to track to its lair this mysterious taint in human experience; this seemingly ineradicable thing called sorrow.

No one in Buddha's time knew how to set up the conditions for a research project. In those days, sages thought about things and talked about them—from the inside; introspectively. The approach to every psychological problem was through meditation. There were no controlled experiments and no sustained observations except upon the nuances of one's own states of mind and body.

Buddha had to fly blind. He tried out experiments on himself—many of them extreme and more or less futile, like trying to live on a few kernels of corn. He wandered about observing people in all their relationships, trying to get hold of the elusive causes of their miseries.

After a while, he made what he thought was a decisive discovery: men are miserable because they desire things; and because desire can never be wholly fulfilled. Desire in man, he concluded, is the cause of human unhappiness. Then he went on with his experimenting and observing. Could one eliminate desire? He tried it out on himself and became his own control experiment.

Buddha's life was ennobled by his courageous persistence in searching for an elusive truth. He never rightly found the truth, because when he discovered "desire" he did not know how to appraise it as part of the growth-pattern of life; he did not see it as something that could be civilized and matured in us. He saw it only as an operative evil to be eradicated.

If Buddha did not discover the truth, he did, however, in the process of trying to eradicate "desire," discover some notable truths. For Buddha's way of getting rid of desire was to outgrow immature egocentricity. His Eightfold Path is a great psychological document attesting to the fact that life-fulfillment is a process of moving away from the illusory satisfactions of ego-absorption toward the genuine satisfactions of whole-relationships: right view; right aim; right action; right speech; right living; right effort; right mindfulness; right contemplation.

"When a man has pity on all living creatures," said Buddha, "then he is noble." Here, as in the case of Jesus of Nazareth, there was mature insight. But it was not long before that insight was institutionalized. Then the inevitable happened. An insight into man's inner maturing became a practice of outer ceremonial, until today the mature wisdom of Buddha has been so crusted over with superstitions that little likeness now exists between Buddhism and the insight of the founder. Buddha was not crucified. His mature insight was crucified.

VI

Today we are uneasy about religion because we note, with a feeling of guilt, that what should unite us has served to divide us; and that institutions that should help us to become immune to the ordinary standards of power and success have themselves made an ill-concealed surrender to those standards. With our guilty religious conscience we try to overcome disunity: we hold interfaith meetings and world congresses of religions.

For the most part, however, in spite of their earnest sincerity, efforts thus to build "unity" are failures—and understandably so. They look for a common denominator among all contemporary religions. But to find a common denominator between religions that, on the one hand, exalt the dignity of man and promote the love of man for man, and, on the other hand, debase man into an everlasting child, a slave of Deity, and a hater of those who "disbelieve" is to find something so empty of content that it has no regenerative power whatever.

Significant unity can be achieved only *among religions that accept the maturing of man as the central aim of life.* Religions that, in however sanctimoniously disguised a form, encourage the mutual enmities of men cannot be "unified" in any significant sense because they are not in themselves agents of unity. Religions of the sword and the stake and religions that insist upon the permanent childlike dependence of man upon an all-powerful and all-commanding Deity have no conception of man as a creature of inherent dignity. They cannot, therefore, induce him to grow into a mature wholeness of life.

Today as of old the admonition is relevant: "Choose ye this day whom ye will serve." Either, in religion, we serve a belief that encourages man's growth or we serve a belief that keeps him immature. The two beliefs are basically and forever incompatible.

Religions, being products of different cultures, naturally differ in all kinds of ways: in their inherited symbols and ceremonials; in the ways in which they express their truths; in vestment, vessel, and architecture. These things are secondary. In relation to them we can show the same courtesy we would exhibit when we enter a home in a foreign land. The furniture of that home is different; the etiquette and language are different; but in their basic humanness, those who live in the foreign home and build their hopes, habits, and affections around it are people like ourselves. We can respect them as people.

It is so with the religions. Differences of outer form make no real difference if at the heart of each religion there is the belief that man is a creature of dignity whose proper destiny it is to grow into maturity of selfhood. We can live happily with any religion that grandly and staunchly holds to this belief. We cannot live happily with any other.

This, then, is the essential thing to seek for: not the least common denominator among religions, but the greatest common denominator. The greatest is love: the principle that unites man; the power that moves him to outgrow his childishness of mind and spirit and to become happily and responsibly mature.

THIRTEEN

WHAT WE OURSELVES CAN DO

GIVEN THE human predicament as we have analyzed it in the preceding chapters, and given the clue-idea of growth into maturity as the way out of our predicament, what, now, about our individual selves? Where do we start? What do we do?

Obviously, the whole issue of our human destiny comes back in the end to our individual selves. Profoundly as we are influenced by the institutions and customs of our culture—forces that took shape long before we were born—there is in all of us a margin for initiative. In some small way, or in some greater way, we can act maturely instead of immaturely. The sum of our mature acts, in each of us and in all of us, may make the difference between a world headed for destruction and a world headed for creative fulfillment.

What can we as individuals do?

In the first place, we can help to create and to sustain

higher expectations about individual life. There is no sense in trying to mature, or in urging others to mature, if we feel that in growing from childhood to adulthood we are moving toward anticlimax. We need to create for ourselves a new and far more enticing image of adulthood.

William Sheldon has described in vivid terms what he calls the "dying back of the brain" in the adult years of a great many adults. "The days of youth teem with fragments of living knowledge; with daring philosophies; morning dreams; plans. But the human mind at forty is commonly vulgar, smug, deadened, and wastes its hours. Everywhere adult brains seem to resemble blighted trees that have died in the upper branches, but yet cling to a struggling green wisp of life about the lower trunk." [1]

This is no inspiring image of adulthood . . . "vulgar, smug, deadened." It is no image likely to make the young envy the old and eager to grow into their own adult status. Middle- and old-age, instead of revealing an increasing power and sense of fulfillment, reveals rather a dampening down; a letting go; a making the best of a boresome bargain. "The observant student of life watches a launching into the world of wave after wave of human beings, each in a little flare of heroic parental sacrifice; he follows the childish years as emerging minds take hold of the world with eager exhilaration; sees the mental flame burn brightly through early youth; feels it flicker a little at about the time of college; and then at last he must stand by helplessly while the young mind

---

[1] William H. Sheldon, *Psychology and the Promethean Will*, p. 3. New York, Harper and Brothers.

struggles in little fits and starts as if caught in the grip of an unseen suffocating force, only to die back in the end to the dull smudge of a coal that did not catch . . . This is the tragedy of the waste of the brain."

Is this what adulthood *has* to be? There is no denying it: this is what, in most cases, adulthood *is*. The psychiatrist, Harry Stack Sullivan, has written of us: "I believe that for a great majority of our people preadolescence is the nearest that they come to untroubled human life—that from then on the stresses of life distort them to inferior caricatures of what they might have been." [2] Robert Frost speaks of one of his adult characters as a "decent product of life's ironing out."

Is this the image of adulthood that we can safely hold before our young people? Is it an image that we can safely hold even before our adult selves? Must we not shape a new image of adult life as a source of greater and greater creative satisfactions?

We cannot, however, make this image out of nothing. In building the image, we have to consider the processes and powers we have to work with. These processes and powers are made clear to us by the linkage concept of maturity we have been developing.

It is good news that our life can grow in power and happiness as it links itself productively to life other than our own: through willed knowledge, through responsibility, through grace and clarity of words, through empathic feeling, through sexual understanding, through philosophic grasp. It is good

[2] *Conceptions of Modern Psychiatry*, p. 27. Washington, D.C., The William Alanson White Psychiatric Foundation.

news that there is for us no fated road to adult dullness; no fated "dying back of the brain."

If the adult brain does die back; if the adult years are a waste and a disappointment, the reason, we now discover, can be found in conditions that have halted the growth of life into linkage with life. We now know that most of these conditions need not exist; that if, in home, school, church, business, politics, or elsewhere, they do exist, we can alter them. We can, in brief, create conditions far more favorable than ever before for the growth of life into a maturity that is a triumph and a fulfillment.

II

Our first need is to realize that every situation in life offers its opportunity for mature or immature responses. We do not have to wait for special occasions.

One member of a family, for example, makes a mistake. This can be an occasion for angry scolding; or for merciless making of fun; or for an abrupt dismissal of the person and a doing of the thing oneself. Or it may be an occasion for recognizing the human capacity to make mistakes and just dropping the whole matter. Again, in a family, there may be conflicting ideas about what to do on a certain evening. This can be an occasion for whining appeal, or petulant disagreement, or refusal to join with any plan not one's own, or dominating command. Or it can be an occasion for a generous putting oneself at the point of view of each of the others in order to find out some way of best agreement. Or, again, opportunity for mature or immature response presents itself when the adolescent member of the family begins to bring home opinions other than those that have been standard in the family. This can lead to repeated occasions where the adults express their shocked disapproval, point out the ridiculousness or the danger of such views, warn the adolescent that he is callow and needs to grow up as they have grown up. Or it can lead to repeated occasions when the adults of the family draw out the adolescent into full expression of his views; listen with honest interest; express honest doubts if they have any; but express them in such a way that the adolescent is given to feel that he has the right to a mind of his own.

These are little things that hardly seem worthy of notice in a solemn treatise on maturity and survival; but it is out of little things like these that the mature or immature atmosphere of our homes is created. Edna St. Vincent Millay tells of the passing of a love that seemed to have no special reason for passing:

> 'Tis not love's going hurts my days,
> But that it went in little ways.[3]

It is out of the small immaturities of response in the small, day-by-day situations that the disastrous immaturity of home life is often created.

Similar small, but really significant, opportunities for response present themselves in the work life. Here is an execu-

[3] From "The Spring and the Fall" in *The Harp Weaver and Other Poems,* published by Harper & Brothers. Copyright, 1923, by Edna St. Vincent Millay. p. 22.

tive who has tried out something that has not succeeded. Will he shift the blame to someone else? Will he minimize the failure? Will he gloom? Or will he cheerfully act like a member of the human race that is known to make mistakes? Or here is a school principal who learns that the son of an important family in the community has not made the grade. All the psychological gods are there waiting to see what he will do. Or here is a teacher who has suffered a severe reproof. Will she take it out on her classes? Or will she, with entire good sportsmanship, make it an occasion for her own inner growth? Again, every teacher is in a position of authority. Between him and his students there is a gap. Will he so love to exercise his authority that he increases the gap—making his students feel small and frightened? Or will he consider the gap as merely functional in the teaching situation and treat all his young charges as though they were equal with himself in dignity and human rights?

Every organization presents opportunities for mature and immature responses. There is, for example, the person who has run for office and not been elected. Does he drop out of things? Sulk in his tent? Say nasty things about the victor? Claim injustice? There is the individual who, for a number of years, has been in the top office but is now superseded. Does he yield gracefully, generously, keep his hands off unless help is asked and then help with good will? Again, the psychological gods are on the alert for the character structure, mature or immature, that is to be revealed.

Social life offers innumerable occasions for putting ourselves to the test. Here is a man who tells "nigger" jokes. Do his listeners laugh uproariously, compounding the offense of turning the Negro into an object of ridicule and contempt; or does at least one of them quietly indicate by some unmistakable word or gesture that he will not be a party to insulting his fellow man? Here is a person who reports something scandalous of a minority group. Do the listeners join in a common savoring of the scandal, or is there someone who quietly asks for the source of the information? Prejudice, hostility, meanness, cruelty—these play in and out of our daily conversations with people. They give maturity its chance to be a "witness unto the Lord."

One important difference between maturity and immaturity is knowing when to raise issues and when not to raise them. On a tablet in front of the Old South Meeting House, in Boston, are words that describe our Revolutionary forefathers as "worthy to raise issues." If they were thus worthy, they were mature. They knew which things were important and which were unimportant.

A person has to be mature to be worthy to raise issues. Most of the small frictions in life that destroy mutual confidence and enjoyment come from raising issues that are not worth raising, and most of the social inertias and timidities that keep our world from moving toward its ideals express a reluctance to raise issues that should be raised. In the home, for example, there are parents who take the easiest way and let things slide when they should not be allowed to slide. In our organizations there are persons who will not take the trouble, or incur the danger, of raising their voices against a majority when a voice of protest needs to be raised.

A mature person knows the important from the unimportant. He is courageous enough to say his say when the say needs to be said; but also wise enough to withhold his say when the matter is too unimportant to merit discussion.

The proving of our maturity requires no special grand occasion. Freud startled the world a number of decades ago by claiming to be able to see important clues to character in mere slips of the tongue. The condition here is similar. Every typical immature or mature response in any situation, however small, is revelatory of character structure. There are no neutral spaces in life. What we do, anywhere and everywhere, is, in some degree, a report on our maturity quotient.

III

The second thing we can do to make clear the image of maturity is to associate ourselves with groups that promote maturing.

This is a sure test of the individual. Is his social life confined wholly to groups that perpetuate various immaturities: groups that make significance for themselves by snobbish exclusiveness; groups that turn life into a perpetual self-indulgence; groups that preach love of man but practice a required intolerance; groups that make undeviating partisan loyalty, instead of undeviating critical thought, the paramount virtue?

Or does he, consciously and with effortful will, join with groups that make significance out of promoting maturity: groups that deliberately seek to overcome the dangerous immaturities of racial and other prejudice; groups that encourage the citizen mind to be critically alive to issues; groups that practice citizenship by active work for community betterment; groups that seek to remove the conditions that hold people back—through poverty, ignorance, slum life, economic injustice, racial discrimination; groups that work for the wiser nurture and education of the young; groups that seek to broaden and deepen the spiritual foundations of life?

It is in the area of our voluntary group organizations that the great battle between maturity and immaturity goes on. In this area the individual finds his best chance to join his own fairly feeble strength with the greater combined strength of those who care about the fulfillment of life. In older centuries, a person of high concern would undergo the discipline of holiness. He would join a holy fellowship, and, in a planned discipline with his fellows of like spirit, would work for "the glory of God." This was an older way of enlisting one's individual efforts with the efforts of a group that strove for the greater fulfillment of life. In modern times the discipline of holiness has largely disappeared among us, and we tend to go our individual ways without the sense of a mission to perform and a disciplined companionship to help in the performing. It may be that in our zeal for secularism, we have cast out the baby with the bath. Or it may be that a new way of holy discipline is being shaped. The monk in his monastery was a dedicated person. But so, today, is the individual who, in a passion for justice to mistreated fellow men, spends days and nights hard at work for laws that will rectify the injustice. So also is the individual who sees the cruel limitations placed upon child life in our cities and works for breathing space and playing space and for a more generous understanding of young lives caught in the meshes of the law. So also is the individual who senses a greater glory that might invest all life, and who, with his like-minded fellows, works for the greater enrichment of life.

Self-dedication and self-discipline may take many forms. The important thing is that the individual lend himself heart and soul to something beyond his own ego-satisfaction. Today he will have no difficulty in learning thus to lend himself. Our times are out of joint; and the call is for "all good men to come to the support" of Man, bewildered, confused, and self-defeated. Just as in older times there were holy fellowships, so today there are dedicated groups consciously created to do the things that need to be done if man is to fulfill himself in mature happiness.

IV

The third thing we need to do in order to make the maturing process come alive is to contrive a plan for the growth of the mind that has breadth and depth and continuity.

One of the fatalities of our culture has been that it has idealized immaturity. Childhood has seemed to be the happy time. Youth, gone almost before it begins, has been looked back upon wistfully as the golden time that never returns.

The reason we have thus idealized immaturity is that, in the main, our only alternative to childhood and youth has been adulthood—*not maturity*. We have seen ourselves taking on the obligations of adulthood without achieving a new significance and a new creative happiness in maturity. The passing of youth, therefore, has seemed to mean a passing into dullness of routine and into the anxieties of a life caught variously in an economic trap. It has not meant for us the entrance into a new dimension of life in which a new and zestful activity of our minds would bring experiences that would more than compensate for the loss of the young years.

The idealization of childhood and youth has tended to influence all our institutions. It has made parents afraid of their children—afraid to set reasonable standards for them lest the children think of them as "old fogies." It has made advertisers able to frighten us into buying by warning us that if we do not buy their products we shall look old: have wrinkled hands, or lackluster teeth, or eyelashes that fail of the seductive upcurve of youth. It has turned education into a sole service of the young. "We want our children to have what we did not have." Thus led to think of adulthood as a time of glory departed, it is no wonder that adults have no buoyant and courageous impulse to seek ways of achieving a new significance in their adulthood. The fact that our culture has not given to adults even a fraction of what through schools, colleges, and universities it so generously gives to children and youth, is a sufficient indication that adults have had no profound belief in the dignity of being adults. The best of their life is over. The rest is a resigned settling down into making a living.

Even such adult education as has been offered to adults has been chiefly aimed at amelioration, not transformation. A course here and there; a bit of craftwork; a hobby—something to enliven a few hours and maybe stir the mind a little. Adult education has never dared to speak out for the right of adults to the kind of education that recognizes *their entrance upon a new and uniquely significant stage of life-experience*. We talk of preparing youth to enter the life ahead of them. We never talk of preparing adults to enter the peculiar new dignity of a *maturing adulthood*.

Yet psychological maturing is our most triumphant way of human fulfillment; and the adult years are the only years in which that triumph can be experienced. Children and adolescents cannot yet experience the mature insight of adulthood. They can only prepare for them. Children and youth, in fact, instead of living triumphant years, actually live years of various frustration. Try as they may, they cannot yet think the mature thoughts and do the mature things that they will eventually be able to do if fortune is kind to them and there is no arrest in their development. Far wiser than the usual idealization of childhood and youth is the insight embodied in the crisp remark of a bright-eyed old lady: "It's a good thing young people are so beautiful, because they have so little else to recommend them."

Adulthood, in brief, is the significant period toward which life heads. It is the time when all the preparings can come to their fruition. Education in the adult years, then, should, by rights, be more than a feeble adding of this course or that to keep the mind busy and reduce its boredom. It should be the kind of education that sets out to do a notable thing: to take us as adults, in this newly arrived time of our life and help us to move beyond the routines of a half-baked adult-hood into the creative surprises of an adulthood that is truly maturing.

As yet we have no such education. There are brave be-ginnings; but they are only beginnings. For the most part adults remain unserviced by the educational institutions of our culture. A falsely conceived *laissez-faire* philosophy keeps up its chant: "Let the old folks look after themselves."

While the chant goes on, and while adults by the millions pass deathward without ever experiencing the triumph of the maturity that should be theirs, we may at least ask ourselves what a lifelong growth of the mind would be like that was undertaken by adults for initiating themselves into their new dignity of life.

V

We can only conjecture. But with our more recent psycho-logical insights into the ways in which life can be robbed of dignity, and the ways in which it fulfills itself, our con-jectures can now have some measure of objectivity.

Imagine a community in which practically all the adults came to a realization of their unfulfilled adulthood. (This indeed requires a high order of imagination!) Imagine the adults in that community agreeing that their adult years should be devoted, as far as other obligations make possible, to maturing their adulthood; to making it a triumph of new significance instead of an apologetic dullness.

What, they would ask themselves, do adults need to know

and do in order to make their adulthood come fully alive? Again, we are only conjecturing; but certain agreements might conceivably be reached.

In the first place, they might agree, adults, having advanced beyond childhood and adolescence, need now to see themselves *with the eyes of maturity*. For the first time in their lives, they possess these grown-up eyes. They need, therefore, to look at themselves and maturely appraise themselves.

This might be accepted as their first adult project. We can imagine them asking experts to come and open up to them the new knowledge about the human mind and character that has been brought to us: psychologists, psychiatrists, physicians, anthropologists, sociologists. They would not speak of this as a "course" in psychology, but rather as their adult attempt at *self-understanding*. They would be making their Socratic beginning: *Know thyself*. It would be immaterial to them whether the expert came from one or another specialized department of learning. All of them together—experts and adults—would be concentrating upon the central issue: *the mature understanding of themselves*.

It is tragic to think that nothing like this takes place in the world today. Nowhere are adults, in sizable numbers and in a community of relationship, *seeking to understand themselves*. Nowhere are the transformative insights of psychological and social research being passed over into lives where they might function. Our culture goes on burying its psychological gold in the Fort Knoxes of specialized scholarship. The group of adults we are imagining would, however, be daring enough to get this gold into circulation.

They would see a second thing they needed to do. Now for the first time they could look back upon their lives and make an appraisal of the ways in which they had been nurtured and educated. With their new self-understanding they could begin to estimate the good or the bad, the wisdom or the folly, of what had been done to them in home, school, college and elsewhere. They would therefore be in a position to judge, with a new wisdom, how all young lives should properly be brought up.

What, they would now ask themselves, should education in the young years be? In seeking the answer to that question, they would be preparing themselves for a wise partnership in bringing up young life in home, school, college, and elsewhere. They would gain an expertness of view in a realm where now adults are mostly ignorant, mostly tenacious of old habits and practices, and too often intolerant of change.

They would want to do a third thing. Realizing from their new psychological insights how profoundly environments influence individual life, they would want to make research into the particular environment that was shaping—perhaps in many ways, misshaping—their own lives, the lives of their children, and the lives of their fellows. They would want to get a frank and intelligent look at their community. They would want to move about their community prepared to estimate what it did to the people who lived in it, and what it needed to do.

They would want, then, to make the difficult approach to the wider world—of the nation, and of the many nations and peoples. They would want to lift themselves out of the illusions and miscomprehensions of their newspaper-made minds and learn something of what lies behind the clutter of unrelated headlines. This would be a notable project. Grounded, by now, in a certain measure of self-understanding and community-understanding, they would no longer see their world as merely one of outer happenings. They would be psychological enough to see their world in its inner motivation—its ambitions and struggles for power; its fumbling efforts at justice and liberation. In short, they would see national and world events, both in their confusion and their clarity, as the inner life of men finding its outer expression.

Finally, they would want to make themselves at home in the great human tradition. They are heirs to that tradition. For the most part, however, because of the prevailing poverty of educational insights and methods—not to speak of lack of time in the school and college years—they will have learned little of what their forefathers willed to them: philosophy, science, religion, poetry, drama, story, heroic acts, brilliant inventions, defeats that were victories. A lifetime would not be long enough for them to take over and put into use this full rich inheritance; but their adult lifetime might well be spent in moving into this inheritance of the spirit.

VI

So much for what this group of maturing adults would try to learn. Inevitably, as the learning went on, the areas of their awareness would be expanded. They would be wiser because more understanding. They would achieve the dignity of individuals unapologetic about their adult years because those adult years were giving them, for the first time in their lives, the chance to see life as only mature eyes can see it.

But learning would be only the beginning. They would want to put their learning into practice.

In the first place, *the practice of creating.* Out of the human tradition they would have caught the flair of man's creativeness. They, too, would want, in some manner, to experience this same creativeness. Whether in music, or poetry, or story-writing, or painting, or sculpture, or craftsmanship, they would want the exciting experience of making the word become flesh.

In the second place, *the practice of obligation.* What they learned would increasingly give them the sense that they were debtors to life. In some measure, therefore, they would feel that they must pay back even a little for value received. They would want, then, each on his own or in fellowship with others, to undertake some project for human betterment, some way of bringing more of reasonableness into the human scene.

In the third place, *the practice of research.* Most adults remain merely adults because they never do more than skim the surfaces of things. They get the habit of being surface-minded; with surface opinions that become surface dogmatisms. These adults of whom we are speaking would want to raise their adulthood above average superficiality by going—each of them—at some specific problem, physical, or social, or what not, and applying their minds in the way that good minds should properly be applied. One sustained experience of rigorous research would make all superficial thinking thereafter tame by comparison.

In the fourth place, *the practice of sociability and of play*. Learning together, they would like the feeling of being together. They would make occasion for coming together, in various self-chosen groupings, for the sake of enjoying one another, and for the relaxation of doing things that have the life-sustaining unseriousness of play.

VII

The foregoing is pure imagination. Such a community of adults, making the effort deliberately to move into the full dignity of their adulthood, may never exist in our world. If so, it will be too bad. Their number ought to be legion; and they ought to spread throughout the nations and peoples of the world. But underlying the pure imagination is sound truth. These are some of the things that adults could learn and do and thereby achieve the fine excitement of being mature men and women.

Brother Lawrence chose to entitle his unpretentious book: "The Practice of the Presence of God." He meant by this that the Life that is most significant in the universe is present in all places and situations—in the scullery as truly as in the cathedral. If we were to coin a similar phrase, we might speak of *the practice of the enjoyment of maturity*. We would mean by this, in similar manner, that there is no time and place in which the adult is exempt from the obligation to practice maturity nor without the power to enjoy maturity. If he responds to a situation with a mind open to learn what needs to be learned, he practices—and enjoys—maturity. If he is ready to act responsibly where responsibility is called for; if he sinks his ego out of sight; if he seeks self-understanding and a wise understanding of others; if he tries to see in whole instead of in part, he practices—and enjoys—maturity.

Maturity, we now know, need be no dull routine of a defeated and resigned adulthood. It can rather be the triumphant use of powers that all through our childhood and youth have been in preparation.

There is a false and a true way of being concerned about what adults need. The false way is to think of aging as a process inherently unfortunate and one whose increasing disabilities must therefore be mitigated. When aging is thought of in this way, we look about for means by which those who grow old can lessen the increasing boredom of their days. We prescribe hobbies for the old.

This, in fact, is an insult to our adulthood. It is as if, in the aging years, all significance drained out of life and only a twiddling of the thumbs remained. The problem in that case would be to find out how to vary the twiddling.

The true way to think of adulthood is to think of it as a stage of life that has a significance no other stage can possess. Adulthood is the time for putting into effect a wisdom about life that childhood and youth are unable as yet even to possess.

This is the dignity of the adult. This is his dignity provided he is a mature adult, not one who, arrested in his development, is marking time in a prolonged adolescence. What adulthood needs is not hobbies for immature grownups, but helps toward significant and happy maturing.

Where there is no vision, we are told, the people perish. Where there is no maturity there is no vision. We now begin to know this. We realize that the evils of our life come not from deep evil within us but from ungrown-up responses to life. Our obligation, then, is to grow up. This is what our time requires of us. This is what may yet be the saving of us.

INDEX

Naomi Wieland
Betty Rue
Larry Gemmell
Ethel McCue
Ruth Cushman
Joan Cushman
Ethel Heuser
Nellie Grace
Jeanne Salmon
Olive Stilwell
Lois Davidson
Dorothy Reiss
Elise Liehrs
Chris Lamborn
Blanche Garrity